RAC
the driving people

How your car works

Your guide to the components & systems of modern cars, including hybrid & electric vehicles

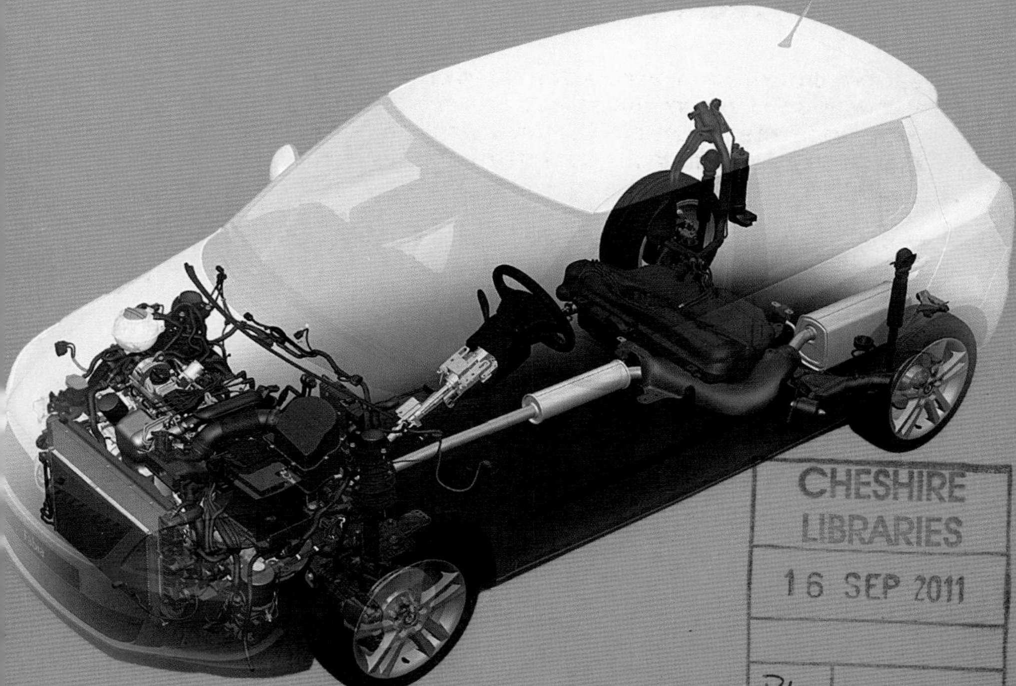

Arvid Linde

Contents

Introduction

The car is undoubtedly one of the most important inventions the world has ever known. Like many other great inventions you cannot pinpoint it to one particular inventor. The car has been a collective effort of many generations of engineers and designers; it has evolved to what it is now thanks to our striving for independence and speed. However, we rarely need to look at the car from a philosophical point of view, and I promise that in this book there will be no long-winded pondering about how cars have shaped the history and direction of our society.

There are people who believe that a car has got a soul, and there are those for whom a car is a mere means of transportation, getting them conveniently from point A to point B. I guess both groups have a valid argument, and it really doesn't matter into which camp you fall. Motoring should be a fun experience, and to make it even more fun and less frustrating, we should try to understand the way our cars work.

Who is this book for? Well, practically everyone who's involved in motoring in one way or another, or anticipates being involved in the near future. This is not one of those typical boys' books – ladies are more than welcome to join in! Whether you're just starting out on the road, or already have some mileage under your belt, understanding your four-wheeled friend can help you both get along much better.

This book is not too technical. However, be prepared to come across a sensible dosage of technical terms from time to time.

We'll start with the outer shell, and then dig deeper to discover the parts, systems, and their working principles …

Arvid Linde
Winner of the *headlineauto*
Rising Star of the Year 2010 (Trade)

one

Car types, construction & body styles

Car types

To begin our fascinating journey through the car, let's familiarise ourselves with the basic layout of several different types of car and what gives them their motive power. Just ten years ago, this chapter would have contained a single cutaway diagram showing what's what in a petrol (gasoline) or diesel engine-powered car. However, car makers have made a big leap forward since then, so now there are three other car types to consider. Hold tight to the steering wheel as we drive through the chapters, unravelling the mystery behind the different systems that make the car work.

Internal combustion-engined car

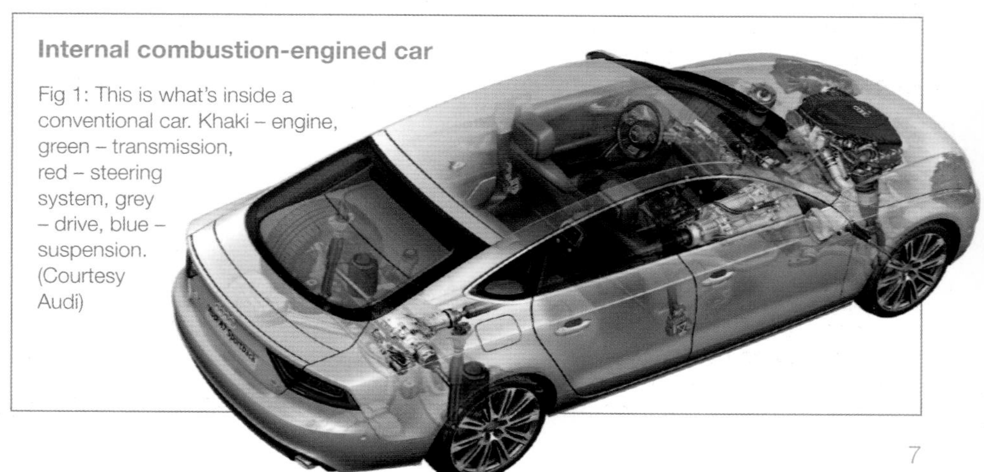

Fig 1: This is what's inside a conventional car. Khaki – engine, green – transmission, red – steering system, grey – drive, blue – suspension. (Courtesy Audi)

Electric car

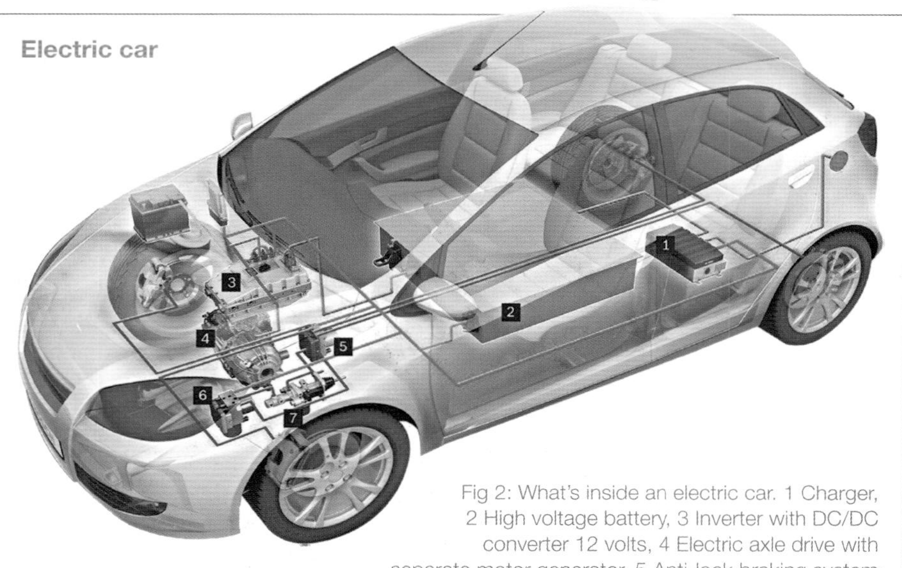

Fig 2: What's inside an electric car. 1 Charger, 2 High voltage battery, 3 Inverter with DC/DC converter 12 volts, 4 Electric axle drive with separate motor generator, 5 Anti-lock braking system (ABS) and Electonic stability programme (ESP), 6 & 7 Regenerative braking system, including actuation control module (6) and brake operating unit (7). Yellow: power supply, Green: communication, Red: high voltage supply, Blue: hydraulic tubes/brake system. (Courtesy Bosch)

Hybrid car

Fig 3: What's inside a hybrid car. 1 Gearbox, 2 Internal combustion engine, 3 Idle shutdown system, 4 Battery pack, 5 Electric motor, 6 Electric power management unit (Courtesy Peugeot)

Fuel cell car

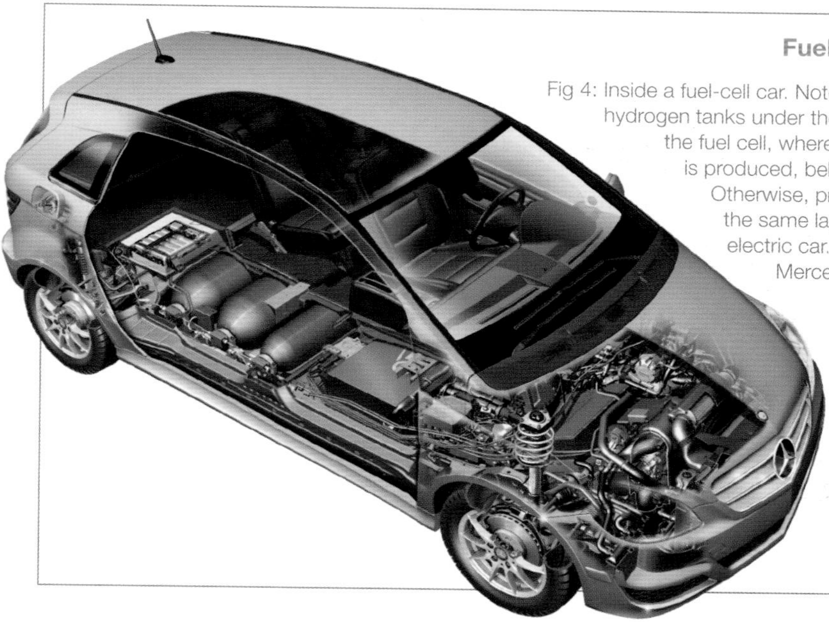

Fig 4: Inside a fuel-cell car. Note the three hydrogen tanks under the floor and the fuel cell, where electricity is produced, behind them. Otherwise, pretty much the same layout as an electric car. (Courtesy Mercedes Benz)

Construction types

There are many ways of building a structure strong enough to support heavy mechanical components, a passenger compartment and the car's bodywork.

Ladder chassis

Fig 5. There are many different ways of building a car, and the oldest one is to start with a ladder chassis, which acts as a platform for the body and provides mounting points for mechanical components, including the suspension.

The 'ladder' name has stuck from early motoring times, because these chassis were made of two longitudinal rails with several horizontal crossmembers. You can imagine

Fig 5: Ladder chassis of a large four-wheel-drive car. (Courtesy General Motors)

that, if you were to lean this type of chassis against a wall, it would actually resemble a ladder.

Although car makers generally began to move away from ladder chassis in the 1950s and 1960s, many still use them for tough four-wheel-drive vehicles capable of serious off-road use.

When it comes to building mainstream cars, however, there are now more efficient methods.

Backbone chassis

Essentially a rectangular 'box' running through the centre of the car from front to rear, forming a backbone to support the car's body and mechanical items.

Such a chassis can be constructed from parallel beams with crossbraces or as a tubular steel lattice. This type of chassis was used by Colin Chapman (of Lotus) when he failed at his first attempt at building a monocoque body in glass fibre.

Tubular spaceframe

Fig 6. A strong favourite with kit car builders and supercar manufacturers, this is a tubular lattice forming a cage-like skeleton.

A tubular spaceframe provides unsurpassed rigidity in all directions. Unfortunately, due to its complexity and a difficult manufacturing process, it is virtually impossible to put into economic mass production. Robotic welders and tubular spaceframes just don't get on too well.

The first production car to be built on a spaceframe was the Mercedes 300SL Gullwing of 1954.

A disadvantage of this structure is the high and wide sills beneath the car doors, which are needed to enclose the tubular framework providing essential strength between the front and rear of the car.

Fig 6: Tubular spaceframe of a two-seater supercar. (Courtesy Lamborghini)

Monocoque

Fig 7. The vast majority of cars built today are monocoques. A monocoque is essentially a chassisless construction and, although the name suggests it comprises one piece (mono means 'alone' in Latin), it actually comprises many sheet metal box structures welded together into a single form.

Computer aided design means that the monocoque can be designed to cope with specific stresses, and can also incorporate areas that will crumple progressively in the event of impact, thus absorbing energy and protecting passengers.

An additional benefit is that the human factor is almost eliminated from car body construction. A carefully planned and programmed conveyor line, 'manned' by robot welders, can produce hundreds of car bodies every day.

Although the majority of monocoques are made of steel or aluminium, or a mix of both (Fig 8), there have been attempts at building carbon fibre alternatives but, so far, not for everyday cars.

Fig 7: Monocoque construction of a modern passenger car. (Courtesy Chevrolet)

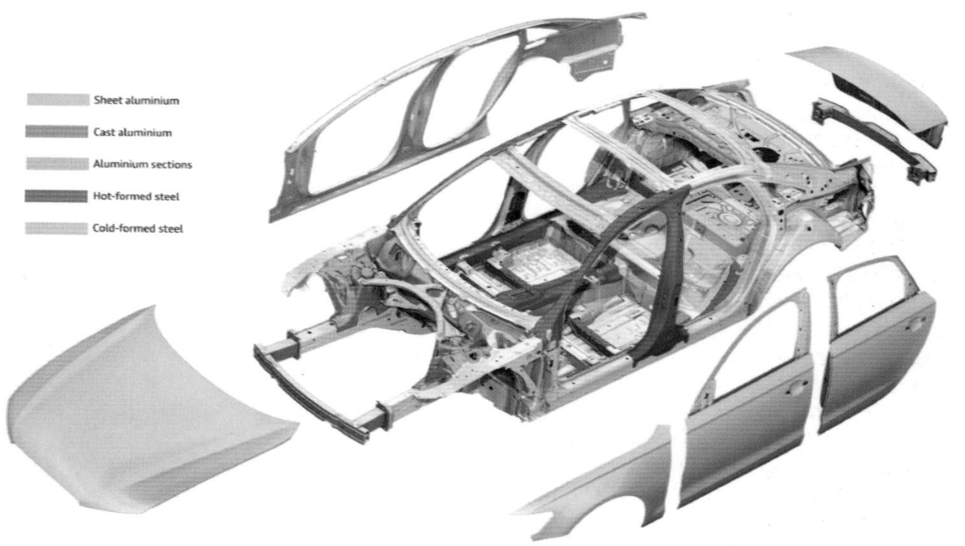

Fig 8: Body construction of Audi A6 showing use of different materials, and a great deal of aluminium to reduce vehicle weight. (Courtesy Audi)

Body styles

4x4/4WD/SUV

Fig 9. '4x4' or '4WD' (short for four-wheel drive) are terms for a passenger cars with four-wheel drive, serious off-road capability and the proportions of a small truck. Americans will more likely use the term 'SUV' (sport utility vehicle) although not all SUV's have four-wheel drive.

These terms are not usually used to refer to four-wheel drive cars like Audi's Quattro.

Convertible

A convertible (Fig 10) is a car with a

Fig 9: A 4x4 car. (Courtesy Land Rover)

Fig 10: A Mazda MX-5/Miata convertible roadster with hood/soft top raised. (Courtesy Mazda)

fabric roof which can be folded down. It can also be applied to cars with folding metal roofs, but these are more commonly called convertible coupés (Fig 11).

Coupé

Fig 12. A coupé is a two-door car with a fixed hard roof. Its body is usually executed in a stylish sporty manner, with a lower rear roofline and sleeker body features. Coupés come as two seaters and four seaters, although in the latter case head and leg room can be restricted.

Fig 11: Peugeot 207 CC (Convertible Coupé) in the process of raising its retractable metal roof. (Courtesy Peugeot)

Fig 12: BMW 3-series coupé. Note the two doors and the sharply sloping rear roofline. (Courtesy BMW)

Fig 13: Volvo V50 estate car or station wagon. (Courtesy Volvo)

Estate car/station wagon

Fig 13. An estate car is a passenger car with an enlarged rear luggage space. Its roofline continues more or less at full height to the rear of the car. Estates are usually four-door cars, with a tailgate (a door right at the rear).

Hatchback

Fig 14. A hatchback is a small car with an opening door at the rear, making it very practical as the rear seat will usually fold forward to create more luggage space. Hatchbacks can come with two or four side doors.

Fig 14: Ford Focus with a hatchback door at the rear. (Courtesy Ford)

Figs 15a & 15b: Fiat Multipla people carrier. Inset shows the seating arrangement. (Courtesy Fiat)

Multipurpose vehicle (MPV)/ people carrier/Minivan

Fig 15a & 15b. These are van-like cars designed to be very flexible with removable and moveable seating. They can be configured to have a large luggage area or enough seating for at least six people.

Saloon/sedan

Fig 16. The British say saloon, the Americans say sedan. This is the typical family car with four doors, four or five seats and a boot/trunk at the rear to carry luggage.

Fig 16: Ford's Mondeo shows how modern saloons are acquiring much more of a coupé appearance. (Courtesy Ford)

two

Propulsion

The propulsion system is the heart of your car; it's what makes it move forwards and backwards.

Ever since Leonardo da Vinci drew a horseless carriage, there have been countless attempts at building the perfect form of vehicle propulsion. If we discount wild ideas, there's really not that much to choose from – steam, internal combustion or electric motor. Each of these three have been used to propel cars. However, it's the internal combustion engine fueled by petrol, gas or diesel oil that has proven the most popular to date, and, although it's not very efficient, the internal combustion engine is here to stay for at least a few more years.

We will ignore steam engines as no mass-produced modern road cars are so powered.

Internal combustion engines

There are various types of internal combustion engines, but it's most likely that your car is powered by a piston engine.

The main parts of a four-stroke piston internal combustion engine

Cylinder block

Fig 17/ item 13. The cylinder block is not only the shell of the engine, but also provides the cylinders within which the pistons travel. Other major parts are attached to it, such as the cylinder head; or operate within it, such as the crankshaft.

The cylinder block also provides mounting points for external components.

If it's a water-cooled engine (the majority of them are), the walls of the cylinder block are hollow to form passages for water to flow through and draw the excess heat away from the

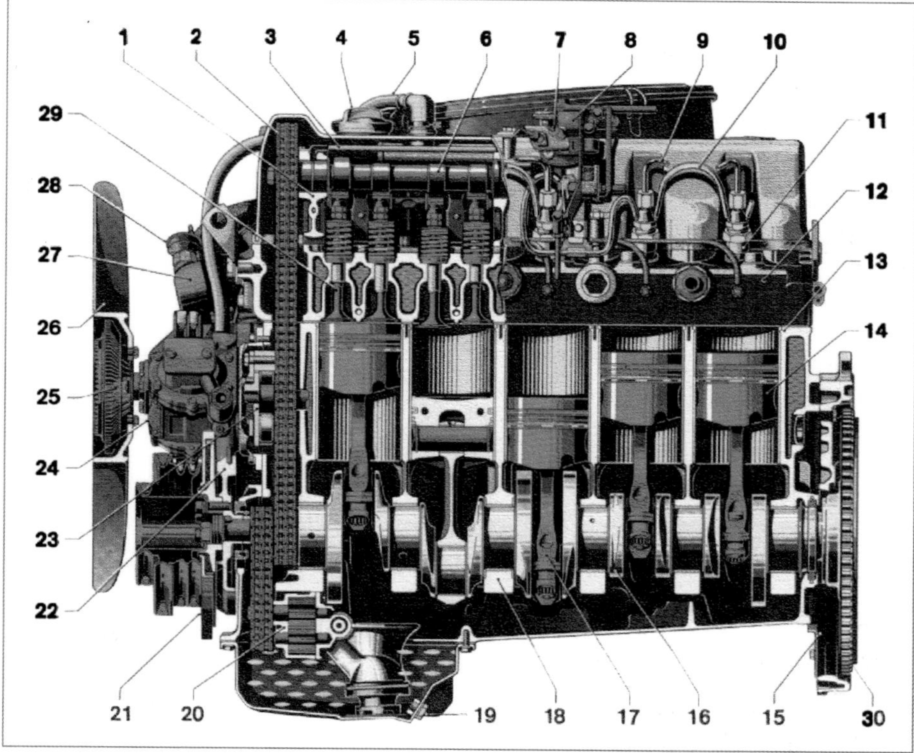

Fig 17: Cutaway view of an internal combustion piston diesel engine (a petrol/gasoline engine is essentially similar in construction, but has different fueling and ignition arrangments. Major components in bold type.

1 Camshaft bearing, 2 Duplex (double row) drive chain, 3 Oil tube (camshaft lubrication), 4 Oil filler cap, 5 Breather hose, 6 **Camshaft**, 7 Cable (idle speed adjustment, 8 Fuel shut-off lever, 9 Fuel pressure line, 10 Fuel return line, 11 Fuel injector nozzle, 12 **Cylinder head**, 13 **Cylinder block**, 14 **Piston**, 15 Intermediate flange, 16 **Crankshaft**, 17 **Connecting rod**, 18 Main bearing cap, 19 Screw plug, 20 Oil pump, 21 Crankshaft vibration damper, 22 Balancing disc, 23 Injection timer, 24 Dual diaphragm vacuum pump, 25 Viscous fan coupling, 26 Fan, 27 Coolant thermostat, 28 Temperature sensor, 29 **Exhaust valve** (**intake valve** adjacent), 30 **Flywheel**.

(Courtesy Mercedes Benz)

upper ends of the cylinders and the combustion chambers.

The cylinder block bolts onto the car's frame. The sump/oil pan, whose purpose is to hold the engine's lubricating oil, is bolted to the underside of the cylinder block below the crankshaft.

Crankshaft

Fig 17/ item 16. Its purpose is to transfer the up and down motion of the pistons into rotation. The crankshaft sits at the bottom of the cylinder block on heavy-duty bearings, and connects to the pistons via connecting rods (remember our cycling analogy). At the front of the crankshaft there are pulleys (wheels with a V-groove around their circumference) or sprockets (wheels with teeth around their circumference) that power different mechanisms via drivebelts or chains.

Flywheel

Fig 17/ item 30. The flywheel is mounted on the rear of the crankshaft. It is a heavy metal disk that performs several functions.

Being a big chunk of metal, once spinning the flywheel stores mechanical energy which helps to prevent the engine stalling at low revolutions, e.g., when changing gear or setting off, and generally smooths engine operation.

When you start the engine, the electric starter engages with a gear wheel running around the circumference of the flywheel (the 'ring gear'), thus turning the crankshaft and starting the four-stroke cycle.

The flywheel also provides the vital link between engine and transmission, as the clutch (manual gearbox) or the torque converter (automatic gearbox), bolts onto its rear face.

Piston

Fig 17/ item 14. The pistons are the driving force behind the whole car. Made of aluminium alloy they are shaped like inverted mugs (without the handles!). Each piston is pushed down the cylinder it occupies by the pressure of expanding combustion gases above its top ('crown'), via the connecting rod, transferring its linear movement into rotation of the crankshaft.

The piston also enables the gas exchange in the combustion chamber to occur, its up and down movement sucking in the combustible mixture and pushing out the exhaust products at different stages of the four-stroke cycle.

The diameter of a piston is always slightly less than the diameter of the cylinder it occupies to allow for expansion caused by heat. However, a significant gap between the piston and cylinder would allow combustion gases to escape past the piston into the sump. This leakage would reduce the force with which the piston is pushed, making the engine weaker. How then to deal with the necessary clearance?

Each piston has several radial grooves where springy metal rings are inserted. There are a minimum of three 'piston rings' per piston, although some engines will have more. The top two rings are called 'compression rings' – they basically keep the piston clearance gap closed, and ensure that the pressure doesn't leak from the combustion chamber to the sump. The lower piston ring is called the 'oil ring.' In all modern engines it consists of several components, and its purpose is to form an oil film on the walls of the cylinder to prevent excessive cylinder bore wear.

Cylinder head

Fig 17/ item 12. Made of cast iron or aluminium alloy, the cylinder head bolts onto the top of the cylinder block. The cylinder head contains the combustion chambers on its underside. It also provides a home for the intake and exhaust valves above every combustion chamber, and mounting points for the intake and exhaust manifolds.

Valves

Fig 17/ item 29. Each combustion chamber will contain ports to allow the intake of a combustible fuel/air mix and the expulsion of exhaust gases. Valves are used to open and close these ports.

Many modern cars will have three or even four valves per combustion chamber to optimise gas flow.

Camshaft

Fig 17/ item 6. Opening and closing of each valve is controlled by the camshaft or camshafts, long and sturdy shafts with eccentric lobes corresponding to each valve. These lobes push the valves out precisely when needed. The camshaft may be directly above the valves or connected to the valves by pushrods and rockers, or just rockers.

The camshaft is driven by the crankshaft, at half crankshaft speed, via a drivebelt or a chain.

OHV, SOHC or DOHC?

OHV: In an OHV (overhead valve) layout the camshaft is located within the cylinder block, and drives the valves from above the combustion chambers via cam followers, pushrods, and rocker arms (Fig 18).

This system is now somewhat outdated because the transfer of power involves so many different stages (camshaft lobe, cam followers, pushrod, rocker arm, valve) the valve train suffers from inertia, making it quite a challenge to precisely regulate valve opening and closing ('valve timing') at higher revs.

SOHC: Stands for single overhead camshaft, meaning a camshaft located in the cylinder head. The camshaft's lobes will often directly push the cam followers, which in turn will push the valves. Unlike the OHV, there are no pushrods and, usually, no rocker arms. An OHC system is more efficient and easier to regulate, permitting higher engine revs than an OHV system.

DOHC: Stands for double overhead cam: a level up from SOHC. There are two camshafts above the cylinder head;

Fig 18: Section cut through a diesel engine illustrates an OHV layout. 1 Pushrod (pushed up and down by the lobes of the camshaft down in the cylinder block), 2 Rocker arm, 3 Paired valves, 4 Valve springs, 5 Combustion chamber, 6 Piston. (Courtesy General Motors)

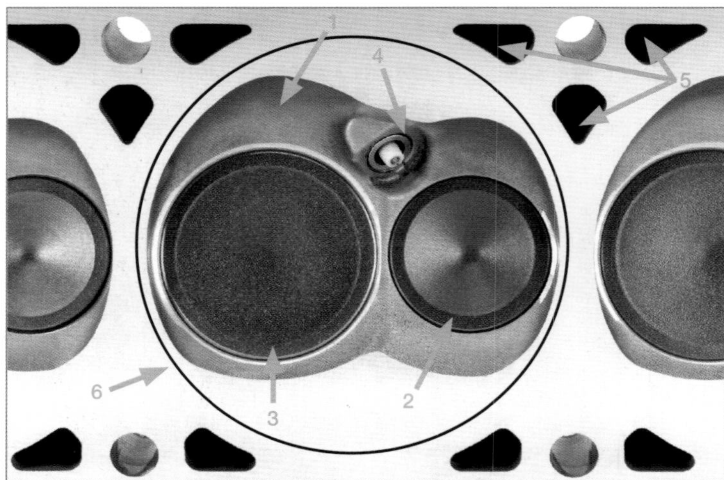

Fig 19: Cylinder head viewed from underneath. 1 Combustion chamber, 2 Exhaust valve, 3 Intake valve, 4 Sparkplug electrodes, 5 Coolant passages, 6 Circle drawn over combustion chamber to represent the top of a cylinder. (Courtesy General Motors)

Fig 20: Section cut through a cylinder head illustrates a double overhead camshaft (DOHC) layout. 1 Camshaft lobes, 2 Rocker arms, 3 Valve springs, 4 Valves, 5 Valve seats. (Courtesy General Motors)

one camshaft driving the intake valves, the other the exhaust valves (Fig 19).

All these traditional means of driving the valve train may soon become history. It is now possible to operate the valves electronically/pneumatically, thus greatly reducing the energy needed to power the valves. Such systems will also allow tremendous precision when it comes to regulating valve timing. Furthermore, it is possible to shut down one or more cylinders when cruising to enhance fuel economy.

Intake manifold
Usually of aluminium alloy, or even plastic, this component is bolted to the side of the cylinder head. The intake manifold contains passageways feeding the combustible mixture to the combustion chambers.

Exhaust manifold
Usually of cast iron, this component is bolted to the side of the cylinder head (usually on the opposite side to the intake manifold). The exhaust manifold provides passageways for exhaust gases to leave the cylinders and enter the exhaust system.

Turbochargers and superchargers

Both are chargers (compressors), also called 'blowers,' used to push more fuel/air mix into the combustion chambers than would be drawn in by atmospheric pressure alone (so called 'normal aspiration').

Turbocharger

Fig 21. A turbocharger consists of two small turbine wheels sitting on the same shaft within a sealed casing. One of the turbo wheels is driven by the exhaust gases rushing by its vanes; this rotation is transferred to the intake turbine which pushes air into the intake manifold at above atmospheric pressure.

This is a very good way of harnessing the energy of exhaust gases which would otherwise simply be expelled to atmosphere. The downside of a turbocharger is that it takes time for the exhaust gases to bring the turbo wheel to its optimal speed – that's why the extra boost is not available instantly the accelerator is pushed. Some turbochargers operate at speeds of 100,000rpm, and it may take anywhere up to several seconds for the turbocharger to 'kick in.' When it does, you'll instantly feel the power surge.

Fig 21: A turbocharger. Powered by the hot exhaust gases racing out of the combustion chambers. The left fan turns the right fan, which sucks air in and delivers it to the intake manifold under pressure. (Courtesy General Motors)

Supercharger

Another method of getting more fuel/air mix into an engine is to use a supercharger. This device is an air compressor driven from the crankshaft via a belt.

A supercharged engine will lose some efficiency, because a certain amount of the extra power generated goes towards running the supercharger itself. On the other hand, an advantage of a supercharger is that there is no lag between pressing the accelerator and extra power being generated.

How an internal combustion engine works

Definitely one of the most important inventions of mankind, the internal combustion engine still powers the majority of vehicles even though it was invented more than 100 years ago.

An internal combustion engine generates power by exploding a fuel/air mixture in a confined space, then converting the resulting gas pressure into mechanical motion. Over the years, there have been attempts to create various different types of internal combustion engines. However, the four-stroke (explanation later) piston engine is by far the most popular.

The theoretical operating principles of a four-stroke internal combustion engine were described by a self-taught German inventor, Nikolaus Otto, in the mid-19th century. He later put his theory into practice, outsmarting all previous attempts at creating an internal combustion engine by making it work well. Essentially nothing has changed over the intervening years: our car engines still operate on the same principles, although now much more efficiently and reliably.

As the name 'four-stroke' suggests, the piston engine operation involves four distinct processes which are constantly repeated.

To understand this process better you can think of a bicycling analogy, where your leg muscles are the pistons, your legs the connecting rods, and the cycle's pedal assembly the crankshaft. These mechanical components are identified in Fig 17.

The combustion chamber is the enclosed space above the cylinder within which the piston moves up and down. The combustion chamber is sealed by two valves, one (the 'intake' valve) opens to let the combustible fuel/air mixture into the chamber, the other (the 'exhaust' valve) opens to let the burnt gases escape from the chamber.

Petrol/gasoline piston engine four-stroke cycle

Fig 22.

1. Intake stroke – The intake valve opens and the combustible mixture is sucked in as the piston travels down the cylinder creating a partial vacuum.

2. Compression stroke – The intake valve closes and the piston travels upwards, compressing the combustible mixture into a very tight space. At this point the crankshaft has made one full rotation. Half of the cycle is complete, but power has not yet been generated.

3. Combustion stroke – As the piston reaches the top of its travel the sparkplug, which protrudes into the combustion chamber, ignites the compressed mixture. The valves are still closed, and now, pushed by the expanding gases that resulted from the explosion, the piston travels down the cylinder forcing the crank to turn (as in our bicycle analogy). At last we have power!

4. Exhaust stroke – The exhaust valve opens and the piston travels back up the cylinder pushing the exhaust gases out past the exhaust valve and into the exhaust system.

The cycle is then ready to repeat. The accompanying diagram shows how the four-stroke cycle operates in a single cylinder. However, car engines have more than one cylinder (usually four, six or eight) as this means that different cylinders can be at different stages in the four-stroke cycle evening out the power delivery.

Diesel piston engine four-stroke cycle

Fig 23.

1. Intake stroke – The intake valve

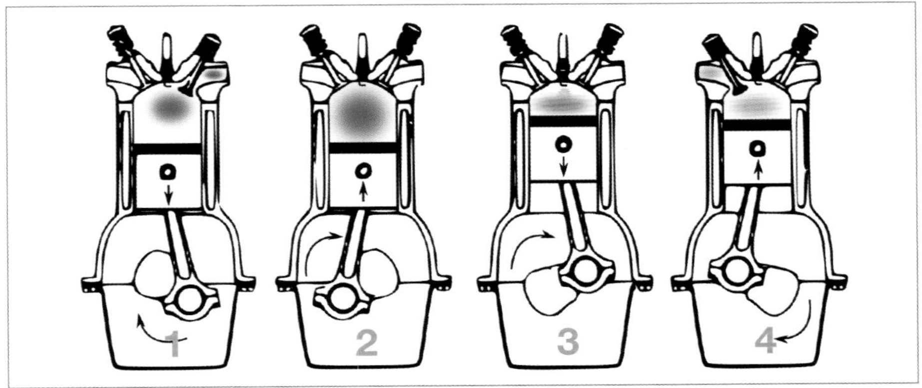

Fig 22: The four-stroke cycle of a petrol/gasoline-powered piston engine.
1 Inlet valve open, piston moving down and sucking fuel air mix into cylinder, 2 Valves closed and piston moving back up compressing fuel/air mix, 3 Valves still closed spark from sparkplug expodes air/fuel mix driving piston down and applying turning force to the crankshaft, 4 Exhaust valve open and rising piston pushes exhaust gas out. Suck, squeeze, bang, blow!

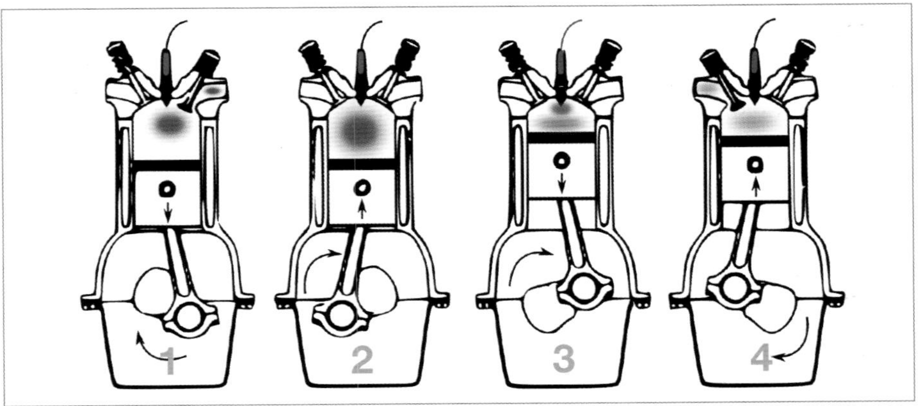

Fig 23: The four-stroke cycle of a diesel-powered piston engine.
1 Inlet valve open, piston moving down and sucking air into cylinder, 2 Valves closed and piston moving back up compressing air, 3 Valves still closed injected diesel fuel ignited by super-heated air expodes driving piston down and applying turning force to the crankshaft, 4 Exhaust valve open and rising piston pushes exhaust gas out. Suck, squeeze, bang, blow!

opens and the combustible mixture is sucked in as the piston travels down cylinder creating a partial vacuum.

2. Compression stroke – The intake valve closes and the piston travels up, compressing the air so much that it heats up to 550 degrees Celsius (1022 degrees Fahrenheit).

3. Combustion stroke – As the piston reaches the top of its stroke the fuel injector shoots in a mist of diesel fuel. Fired by the hot air, the fuel/air mix explodes. The valves are still closed, and now, pushed by the expanding gases that resulted from the explosion, the piston travels down the cylinder forcing the crank to turn (as in our bicycle analogy). At last we have power!

4. Exhaust stroke – The exhaust valve opens and the piston travels back up the cylinder, pushing the exhaust gases out past the exhaust valve and into the exhaust system.

Other differences between petrol/gasoline and diesel engines

Firstly, petrol/gasoline and diesel fuel are entirely different, and therefore so is the fuel system on both types of engine. Secondly, the diesel engine is built to withstand higher internal loads. It has to be able to compress the fuel/air mix more than a petrol engine in order to ensure compression is sufficient to create spontaneous combustion. Therefore, the engine walls are thicker, and the piston rods and crankshaft bearings much stronger than on a petrol/gas engine.

Because it is built in a more substantial manner and is a low revving engine, the life cycle of a diesel engine is generally much longer than a petrol/gas one.

A diesel engine is more eco-friendly because its cycle is more efficient, which is why it requires less fuel to generate a certain amount of power.

On the other hand, a petrol engine is generally more responsive and has a broader power band.

Rotary engines

A rotary engine doesn't have any pistons. It doesn't have valves, either. Instead, it has a number of triangular rotors on a crankshaft, each turning inside a specially shaped chamber, and acting as both piston and valve (see Fig 24).

The concept of rotary engines is quite old: it was the German inventor Felix Wankel who made the idea workable in 1957. It took him more than 30 years to get there, but the result was well worth it. The Wankel engine is one of the very few alternative engines ever produced on a mass scale.

Because the rotor makes orbital movements around the shaft, this kind of engine runs very smoothly.

During a single revolution, each face of the rotor should make a full power-producing cycle, going through an intake phase, a combustion phase, and an exhaust phase. Compared with a piston engine, less movement is necessary to produce power, there is less friction, and fewer moving parts, all of which make a rotary engine more efficient than a piston engine. This efficiency allows a much more compact powerplant for any given output.

Traditionally, the sealing units (at the apexes of the rotor) have been known to play up, causing compression loss and high fuel consumption. However, according to Mazda, this problem has now been eradicated.

Electric propulsion

There's no denying that electric cars will be an important part of our motoring future, particularly for city dwellers.

An electric motor converts electrical energy into mechanical energy, and is really a very simple device. At its most basic level, it has just two components, and only one of them moves.

Apart from the motor, there are other important parts making the electric car work. The motor controller is a computerised device that monitors the motor's speed, power consumption, and temperature. The signals from the accelerator pedal are sent to the

Fig 24: A rotary engine. 1 Rotor, 2 'Crankshaft,' 3 Combustion chamber, 4 Exhaust outlet, 5 Intake port. (Courtesy Mazda)

controller, which determines how much direct current should be taken from the batteries, converted to alternating current, and used to drive the motor.

The electric car doesn't need a traditional gearbox, so no gear changing is necessary. Direct current (DC) motor-powered cars do need a simple gearbox that allows them to shift into reverse. However, except for home builds, DC is gradually being phased out. An AC motor can run in the reverse direction at the touch of a button.

An electric car needs rechargeable batteries as a source of energy. The best batteries for this purpose use the same technology as your mobile phone's battery, yet the electric car's batteries will amount to a considerable weight if they are to provide the car with a reasonable travel range. Batteries that can provide enough energy for a 160 kilometre/100 mile travel range will weigh at least 160kg/350lb, not counting the safety equipment that goes with the battery pack.

Lead-acid batteries, like the one used to start your conventional car, can be used to power electric cars, but they are relatively heavy and inefficient.

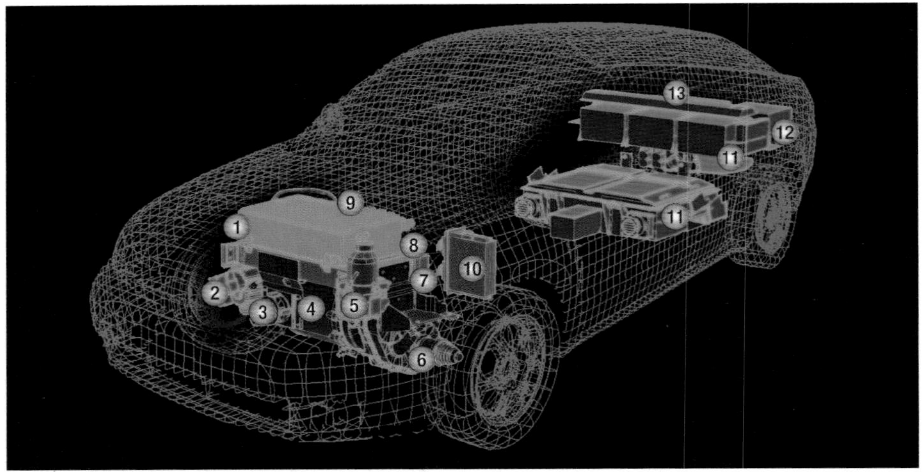

Fig 25: Major components of an electric car's propulsion system – see text for key. (Courtesy Ford/Magna International)

Major components of an electric car's propulsion system

Fig 25. The illustrated example is a front-wheel drive car. Not all of these components are obligatory for a very basic electric car; however, a more advanced car will have more components than those mentioned here.

1. Motor controller.
2. Air-conditioning system.
3. Electric water pump that circulates the coolant necessary to carry away whatever little heat there is in the electric motor and batteries. There is not a lot to cool, though.
4. Electric motor.
5. Power steering mechanism.
6. Reduction gear (electric motors spin very fast!). In Ford's case the reduction ratio is 5.4:1.
7. Powertrain cradle that fixes the motor to the chassis via flexible, anti-vibration, mountings.
8. Electric vacuum pump that powers the brake system and power steering.
9. High voltage electric heater. This is how the car's interior is heated.
10. Vehicle control unit – the 'brain.' It monitors and controls everything in the propulsion system starting with regenerative braking and ending with power distribution between the two driving wheels.
11. Battery pack. The amount of battery cells depicted contains 23kWh of energy, good for covering roughly 160km/100 miles between recharges.
12. AC charger. The battery needs DC (direct current) to charge but you'll be plugging your car into an AC (alternating current) supply. The charger's task is to convert AC to DC.
13. DC to DC converter. This converter supplies electricity from the main battery pack to charge a single 12V battery that is used to power headlights and other ancillary devices.

How an electric motor works

There are two types of electric motor – direct current (DC) and alternating current (AC). Direct current means the supply of electricity is constant, alternating means the supply is effectively switched on and off, on and off, in a very fast sequence.

Although the DC system is much simpler, 95 per cent of the factory-made passenger electric cars are powered by an AC motor because it is more efficient. On the contrary, the vast majority of home-made electric car conversions use a DC system as it can still provide decent power and is much cheaper.

It is important to grasp the basics of magnetism in order to understand how electric motors work. If you take two magnet bars marked with positive and negative poles and put their positive ends together, you would see that they repel each other. If you bring the opposite ends together, they are attracted to each other. This phenomenon is the natural force employed in the operation of an electric motor: one magnet (the 'rotor') rotating inside another fixed magnet (the 'stator'). See Fig 26.

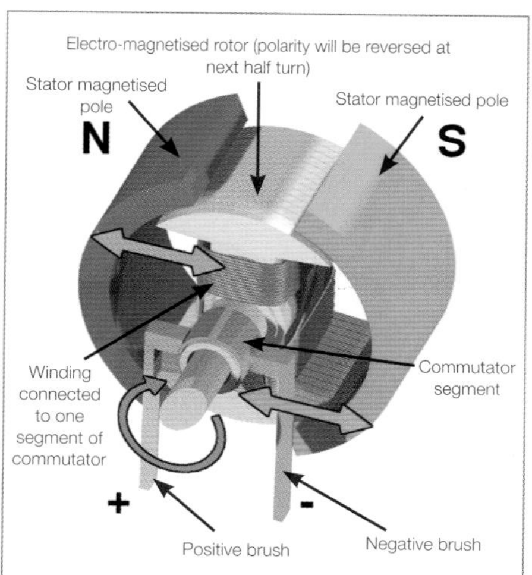

Fig 26: Simplified electric motor shows how rotor segment with the same magnetic pole is repulsed by stator area with the same pole.

The battery electrical supply is connected to the individual brushes of the electric motor, thus their polarity is always constant – one is positive, the other negative. The brushes are in a direct contact with the commutator segments which are each connected to wiring around one section of the armature. As shown in our simple

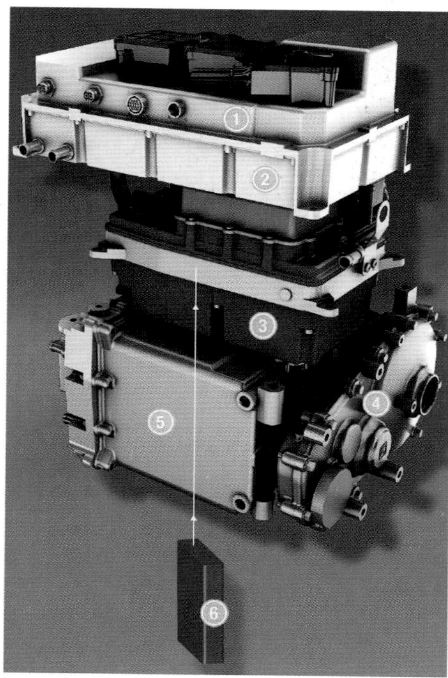

Fig 27: The power unit of an electric car. 1) Junction box (power current distribution and relay for fast charging), 2 Charger (current transformer for battery supply), 3 Power electronics box (power invertor for engine supply and control/transformer for 14-volt network supply, 4 Reducer (replaces gearbox and operates at a fixed reduction ratio), 5 Synchronous electric motor (max speed: 12,000rpm, power: 50-70kW, efficiency: 95 per cent), 6 Supervisor (communications between engine electronics and external elements: ie, battery, vehicle, driver's actions). (Courtesy Renault)

Fig 28: An electric car topping up at a public charging point. (Courtesy Electromotive)

illustration, when the electric motor is switched on, its rotor makes its first half turn as the section of the rotor with the same polarity as the adjacent stator pole is repulsed. At this point the commutator now has different segments in contact with the brushes, which changes the polarity of the same section of the armature so that it is now repulsed by the next section of the stator which has the same magnetic pole, and thus creates a full revolution. This process is constantly repeated.

Want the motor to rotate faster? Just increase the voltage. Want more torque? Increase the current (amps). Want it to rotate in the opposite direction? All you need do is swap the poles. All this means that an electric car doesn't need a gearbox and there is no need to shift the gears, because the torque output of an electric motor is almost constant, regardless of the revs.

Brushless electric motors are available. Although brushes and commutators are very simple, brushes wear and eventually need to be replaced. A brushless electric motor solves this problem by employing an electronically controlled commutator, which will swap armature polarity twice per revolution.

Hybrid propulsion

Although the term 'hybrid' can represent any vehicle powered by more than one source, the word is typically used to denote a car that has an electric motor and an internal combustion engine. A modern hybrid car can switch between using its electric motor and internal combustion engine, or even use both simultaneously, depending on the terrain, driving mode, and available energy.

Fig 29: A plug-in hybrid car of the future. (Courtesy Toyota)

The original concept of a hybrid vehicle was to make internal combustion-engined cars more efficient by collecting the waste energy from braking. At the point that you hit the brakes, your car still possesses a significant amount of kinetic energy, which is wasted unless there's a system to capture and store the energy so that you can use it later. An electric motor is a great option as it can also work as a generator. On a hybrid vehicle, the wheels turn the electric motor all through the braking distance. The current that is generated is deposited in a battery, and you can later use this energy to power the electric motor and drive the wheels.

Another function that makes modern hybrid vehicles more efficient than conventional cars is the idle shutdown system. Normally, when you stop, say, at traffic lights, the engine enters the idle mode, using only as much fuel as is needed not to stall but some fuel is still consumed. However, you were to switch the engine off each time you hit a red light, driving would become a nightmare.

On many modern hybrid cars, there's a system that manages stop-starting for you. The engine is automatically turned off, as an electric motor can provide great acceleration, it will power your car forward when the traffic light turns to green; a few moments later the internal combustion engine is switched back on, and you continue as before. The best thing about the idle shutdown system is that, if it's executed properly, you don't even notice that the engine has stopped working. Acceleration and driving is still smooth and pleasant, however, you save fuel each time you stop.

Hybrid technology makes it possible to use a relatively small internal combustion engine. In fact, when cruising at a steady speed, we don't need much power. The power boost is only needed when we accelerate or tackle a hill. An electric motor is

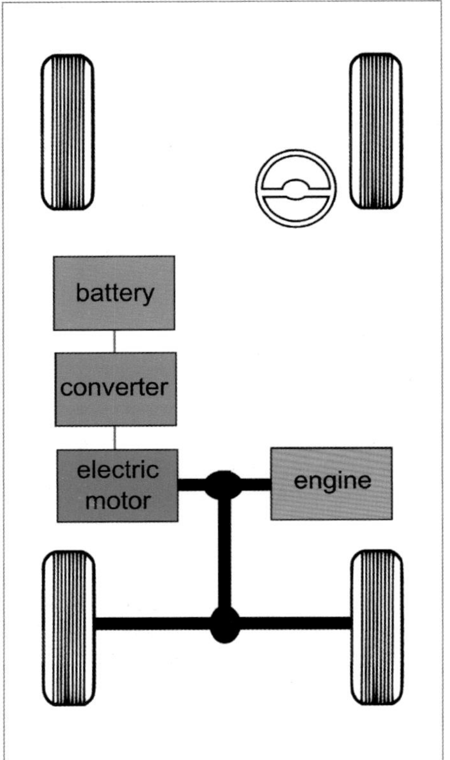

Fig 30: A system schematic of a parallel hybrid car layout. Could also be front-wheel drive.

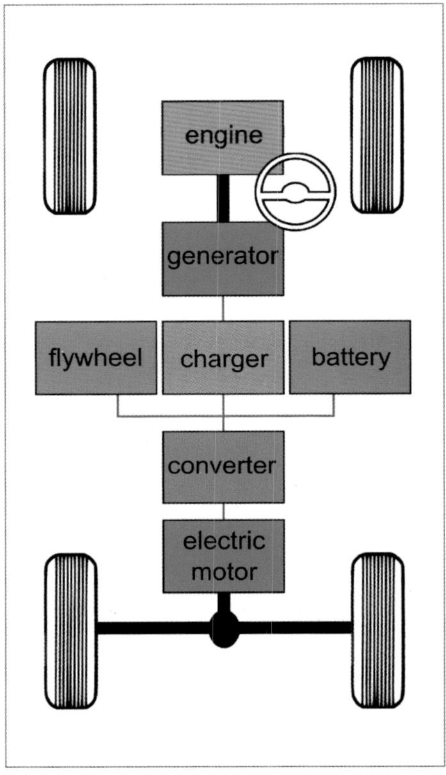

Fig 31: A system schematic of a series hybrid car layout. Could also be front-wheel drive.

perfectly suited for accelerating the car because it produces great torque (muscle power), even at low revs.

Plug-in hybrids are a further step up the ladder of fuel efficiency. Their battery pack can be charged from an external power source (wall socket/on-street charger), and provide a dozen or so miles in all-electric mode, without the engine even starting.

Although mass-production hybrids currently use petrol (gasoline) engines, sooner or later there will be diesel-electric hybrids, making the whole system even more appealing. So far, diesel-engined hybrid cars haven't been viable because they are heavy and difficult to make compatible with an electric motor, due to their relatively low revolutions. However, as diesel engines become smaller and lighter, a diesel-electric hybrid is now a possibility.

According to power distribution and drive train configuration, the hybrid cars can be divided into three groups:

Parallel hybrid

Fig 30. The parallel hybrid has an electric motor and an internal combustion engine connected together via a mechanical transmission. It means that both the engine and the electric

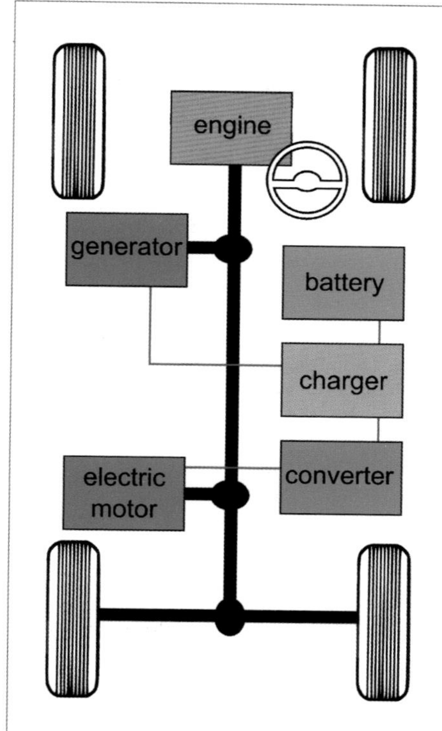

Fig 32: A system schematic of a power split hybrid car layout. Could also be front-wheel drive.

motor can supply power to the wheels simultaneously. They can also work independently. All the ancillary systems like air-conditioning and power steering are powered by small electric motors taking power from the battery pack. This significantly increases the efficiency of the internal combustion engine as there are no more drive belts or chains robbing its power.

Series hybrid

Fig 31. A series hybrid has an internal combustion engine that cannot drive the car's wheels. The Chevy Volt (known in Europe as Vauxhall Ampera) is a series hybrid. The Volt is an extended range vehicle powered by a 120kWh electric motor. Its battery capacity is limited in size: the main block has just 8kWh capacity, providing just 40 miles in the all-electric mode. After the battery is exhausted, an onboard internal combustion engine-powered generator starts up to generate electricity for the electric motor, which then continues to power the vehicle.

Power-split hybrid

Fig 32. There is also a hybrid between the two aforementioned systems. A hybrid hybrid? These cars incorporate features of both parallel and series hybrids. The internal combustion engine can directly turn the wheels, but it can also drive a generator to make electricity. The electric motor can drive the wheels itself, be used in tandem with the internal combustion engine to give a power boost, or can act as a generator and produce electricity when the car is braking.

Alternative propulsion systems

LPG (Autogas)

Fig 33. LPG (liquid petrol gas) is a widely available alternative fuel. In the USA it is sometimes referred to as autogas. Depending on the country, it is either liquefied propane gas, liquefied butane gas, or a mix of the two.

LPG can be burnt in a conventional petrol (gasoline) engine with only minor modifications to the engine. The main reason people choose to convert their petrol cars to accept LPG is the cost effectiveness. Once the capital cost is recovered, these conversions have the potential to halve your car's fuel bills. Also, LPG is a little bit greener than petrol/gasoline: using LPG can cut up to one fifth of the usual CO_2 emissions.

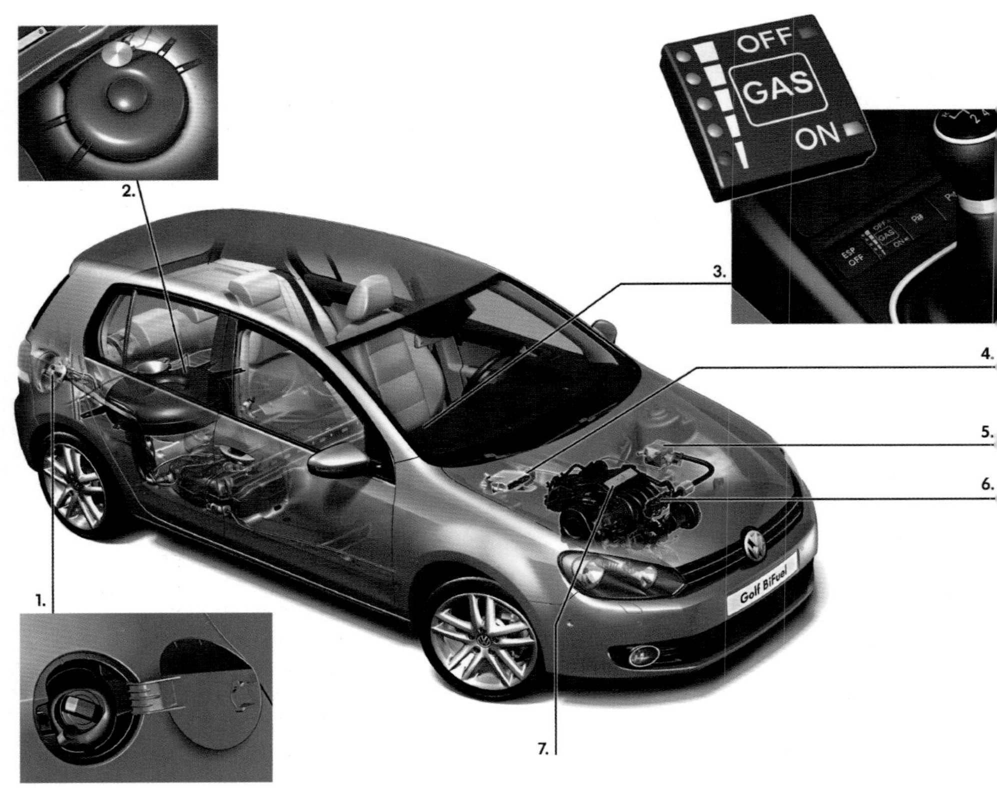

Fig 33: This is no aftermarket conversion. The Golf BiFuel is actually made to be an LPG vehicle. 1 gas filler, 2 gas reservoir, 3 switching between fuels made easy, 4 control unit, 5 evaporator, 6 fuel nozzles, 7 engine. (Courtesy Volkswagen)

Propane and butane are quite easy to source – they are simply a by-product of oil refineries. However, a problem with LPG in some areas is that not every fuel station will have it for sale. Nevertheless, there's always petrol/gasoline-mode at the end of a switch on your dashboard as, in effect, converted cars are dual fuel vehicles.

Because the energy density of LPG is lower than that of petrol (calculated per unit), for the distance you'd cover on one litre of petrol, you'd need 1.2 litres/0.263 imperial gallon/0.317 US gallon of LPG.

Essentially an LPG conversion consists of a tank for the gas, an external filler valve, pipework to the engine and an electronic control unit that plugs into the car's own onboard computer and works in harmony with it. A dashboard mounted control switch is added to make an easy transition between the LPG and petrol.

Biodiesel

Biodiesel fuel can be made from a range of vegetable-based oils, animal fats and waste fats through the process of alcoholysis (treating oil/fat with ethanol). It is truly amazing the range of various substances that can be easily converted into biodiesel, which has similar properties to conventional diesel fuel. However, it can contain impurities, and it can degrade certain types of plastic used in fuel hoses and other parts.

Although many modern cars can use 100 per cent biodiesel safely, older cars (pre-1995) will need to have all non-metallic parts that come into direct contact with fuel replaced by equivalent components made of fluoroelastomer rubber, or other suitable synthetic material.

The manufacturers of high-pressure common rail diesel engines warn motorists against using 100 per cent biodiesel, but have nothing against the 5 to 20 per cent biodiesel mix found in conventional diesel fuel.

So, if you're driving a late '90s diesel car, in many cases you can simply switch to biodiesel without any further considerations, apart from the fact that during the winter months your fuel may turn into jelly. However, please consult a specialist before you do. There are some cars that won't be too happy to have a higher concentration of biodiesel.

There is great potential in biodiesel as it can be made from various crops. For example when growing rapeseed for biodiesel, one hectare of land normally produces 1000 litres of fuel. Farming activity only consumes 82 litres per hectare, so there are 918 litres of surplus every season. Having said that, rapeseed may not be the most efficient fuel crop. Certain types of algae can produce more than 3000 litres of biodiesel per hectare, and palm oil as much as 4500.

For the future, the most appealing method of producing enough biodiesel is mastering an efficient algae growing/harvesting system, and waste oil recycling.

A different kind of eco-friendly diesel is the so-called 'waste oil conversion.' It is quite simple, consisting of an extra tank to hold waste cooking oil, a heater that will heat the contents of the tank (otherwise it will turn into jelly when it's cold outside), and a valve that will mix it with the standard diesel fuel being fed to the engine. If the fuel filters are changed on a regular basis, no harm can occur to the engine.

Ethanol

Ethanol or grain alcohol can be used as a fuel in petrol (gasoline) internal combustion engines. The most popular method is to add ethanol to the petrol in the ratio one part ethanol to nine of petrol. Using this 10 per cent ethanol fuel mix doesn't require any modification to the engine, although it is not recommended for older cars with carburettors. In the UK 5 per cent ethanol in fuel station petrol is permitted.

There is also 'E85' fuel, which contains 85 per cent ethanol and only 15 per cent petrol. In order to use E85, it is likely that some modifications will have to be made, even to modern fuel injection cars. Consult the car manufacturer.

A slight worry is that ethanol has cleaning properties and will loosen deposits in the fuel lines. However, just replacing the standard fuel filter after the first couple of weeks, followed by another change at 2000 miles, and then just carrying on as usual should be fine. Be aware that, as with biodiesel, ethanol can harm the fabric of fuel lines on older cars.

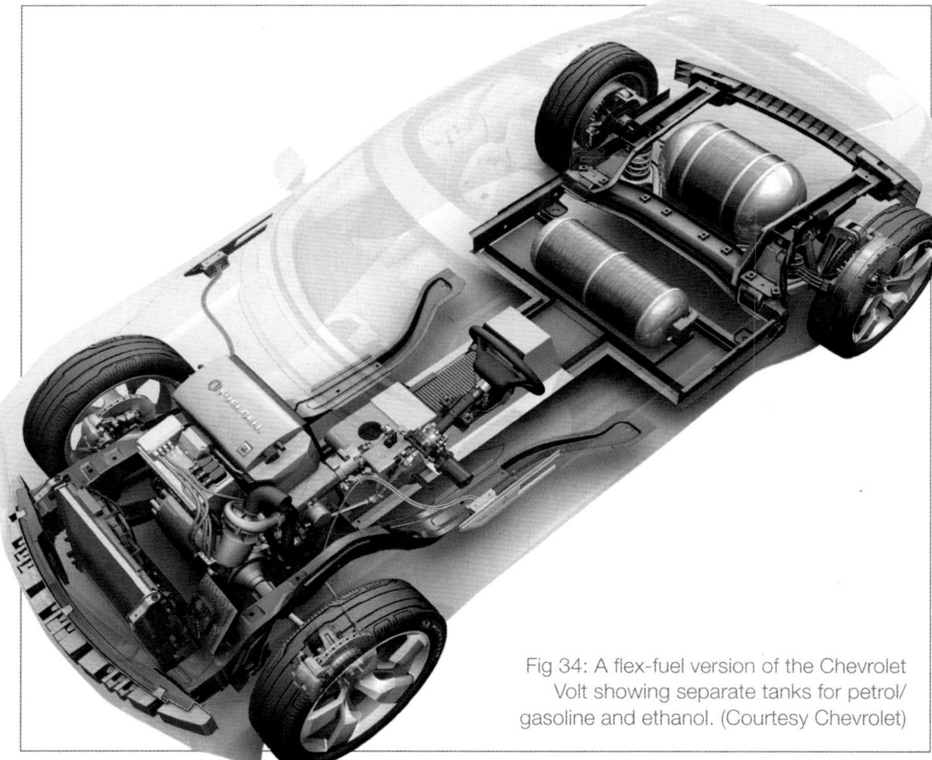

Fig 34: A flex-fuel version of the Chevrolet Volt showing separate tanks for petrol/gasoline and ethanol. (Courtesy Chevrolet)

Flex fuel vehicles

Fig 34. Flex-fuel vehicles can run on petrol (gasoline), ethanol or a mixture of the two – in any concentration. Sensors detect the fuel mix and adjust sparkplug timing accordingly.

It is possible to convert almost any car into a flex-fuel vehicle. The conversion costs have the potential to pay for themselves within the first year of operation, because ethanol is so much cheaper than petrol (at least in some countries). For the majority of us, ethanol is simply not accessible. However, in the USA and some South American countries, the flex-fuel industry is absolutely huge.

The main difference between a bi-fuel and a flex-fuel vehicle is that a bi-fuel car cannot use both types of fuels simultaneously, whereas a flex-fuel one can. For example, an LPG conversion is a bi-fuel vehicle. You can run the engine on petrol or switch to propane – however, it's not viable to mix petrol with propane.

Fuel cells

Fig 4, chapter 1. A fuel cell produces electricity from elements that are fed from an external source. The process that takes place inside the cell is reverse 'hydrolysis' (turning water into hydrogen and oxygen) – instead it turns oxygen and hydrogen into water. The resulting chemical reaction creates electrical current and clean water – the only by-product of a fuel cell. The electricity produced can then be used to power an electric motor, with the excess stored in a 'li-ion' (lithium-ion) battery.

There's plenty of oxygen around in the air, but how do you get a supply of hydrogen? It has to be carried onboard in a high-pressure container in liquefied form.

The problem with hydrogen is that large amounts of electricity are required to make it via hydrolysis. The most eco-friendly method of producing hydrogen is to extract it from ... ahem ... urine, or to employ special hydrogen-producing bacteria. Neither of these two methods have become economically viable on a large scale yet. Once they are, however, hydrogen will make a perfect fuel, so watch this space.

There are very few hydrogen filling stations around the world. There are some in Germany, Switzerland and the US.

Hydrogen

It is possible to burn hydrogen in an internal combustion engine just like normal fossil fuel. You can also build a bi-fuel engine that can switch from petrol to hydrogen on the go. Mazda has been toying with the idea of a hydrogen rotary engine for a few years now. According to Mazda's engineers, the rotary engines are particularly suited to run on hydrogen because they do not suffer from backfiring and misfiring as piston engines do. This is because the rotary engines have separate chambers for intake and combustion, and two fuel injectors per intake chamber.

As in the case of fuel cell-powered cars, you actually need to carry a tank of hydrogen onboard. Also, less power gets to the wheels. With the Mazda Renesis rotary engine in petrol mode its output is 210bhp, while in the hydrogen mode the power is reduced to 109bhp.

Starting system

At the dawn of the motoring era, starting an engine was anything but effortless. The manual starting system consisted of a crank arm that had to be engaged with tangs in the end of the crankshaft, and then be heaved upon with all one's might. It was very difficult, and potentially dangerous.

Although electricity was already available when the first cars were made, it wasn't until the late 1920s that the mainstream manufacturers switched to building cars with electric starters. Some of them continued making cars with both electric starters and a crank arm well into the 1970s.

The starting system of a modern car consists of a battery, ignition key/button, solenoid and an electric starter motor. When the ignition key is turned, or the starter button pressed, electrical current flows to a solenoid which then allows a high amperage current to flow to the starter motor. The starter motor's output gear engages with the ring gear of the engine's flywheel and turns the crankshaft, thus setting the engine in motion.

The solenoid is an electro-mechanical switch that closes an electrical circuit and connects the starter motor to the battery. Because it is electro-mechanical (the electric charge creates a magnetic field which forces a plunger to change its position) the solenoid can also be used to move the starter's pinion (a small gear wheel) into engagement with the flywheel ring gear.

The starter is a simple DC electric motor (please refer to the section about electric cars for more information on how it works).

A traditional lead-acid battery is still used to store the power necessary to start the car and run the ancillary

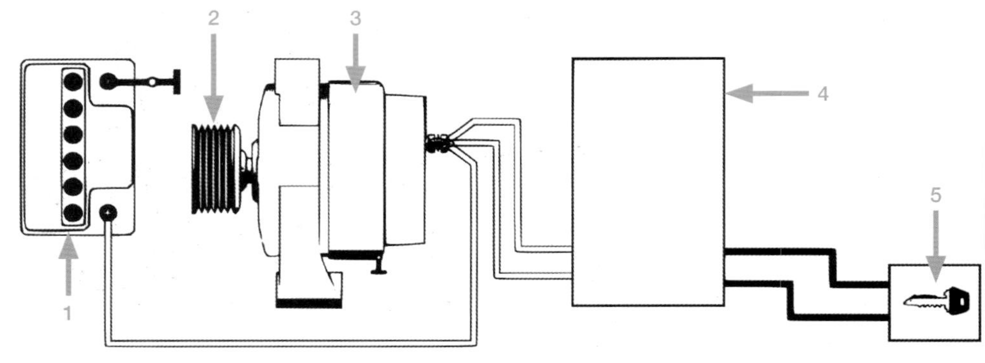

Fig 35: 1 battery, 2 pulley driven by a belt from the crankshaft pulley, 3 alternator, 4 control unit, 5 ignition key. (Courtesy vaz-avtos.ru)

equipment. Although lead-acid technology is extremely outdated, it is cheap and reliable enough not to need to be replaced by more up-to-date battery technology.

Charging system

Fig 35. The charging system is designed to recharge the battery after it has been depleted by cranking the engine. It also supplies electricity to ancillary systems while the engine is running and driving the alternator, the latter being the main part of a charging system. The system includes a voltage regulator, charge level indicator, wiring and the battery.

Technically, an alternator is an electric motor, similar to the starter motor. Its operation, however, is the complete opposite. While the starter consumes electricity to be able to turn, the alternator is driven by the engine to generate electricity. That's the beauty of an electric motor – it will work both ways. If you turn it quickly enough, the magnetic field between the stator and rotor will produce electricity. And the alternator is actually turned very quickly – it is powered by the engine through pulleys and a belt. The belt is driven by a pulley on the front end of the crankshaft.

Fuel system

Fig 36. The fuel system ensures that fuel gets safely from the fuel tank to the engine's fuel distribution device. The main parts of a fuel system are the fuel tank, fuel lines, fuel pump, fuel filters, and a distribution device.

Fuel system of a petrol (gasoline) engine

Fuel tank

The size of the fuel tank is largely what determines the car's range. A normal fuel tank will usually hold 50 to 100 litres/13 to 22 Imp. gallons/16 to 26.5 US gallons. It is usually located at the rear of the car, either under the luggage compartment floor or under the rear seats, and is well protected from

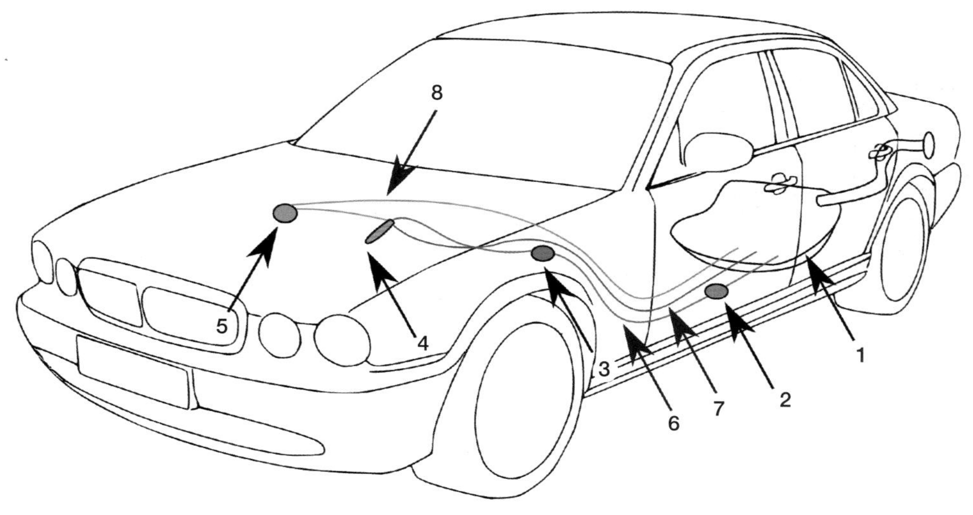

Fig 36: Fuel system of a petrol/gasoline car. 1 fuel tank, 2 fuel pump, 3 fuel filter, 4 fuel injector, 5 vapour canister, 6 fuel line, 7 fuel return line, 8 vapour return line.

collision damage by being tucked away well within the body of the car. The fuel tank is connected to the outside world via a filler neck and a sealing cap.

Fuel pump/pick-up
A fuel pump/pick-up unit is housed in the tank. Its function is to suck the fuel and, sometimes, to gauge the fuel level in the tank. The main fuel line connects the pickup unit with a fuel distribution device on the engine.

A fuel pump is necessary to ensure the constant flow of fuel inside the supply and return pipes. Modern engines with fuel-injection systems use a high-pressure electric pump inside the fuel tank, or even two consecutive pumps – one inside the tank and another closer to the engine.

Fuel pipes (lines)
Fuel pipes (lines) are predominantly made of metal, although with the advance of modern materials, plastic lines can be used to reduce the weight of the fuel system. Where there's the most vibration, near the engine, flexible pipes are used. Nowadays flexible fuel pipes are made of fluoroelastomer-based material.

In modern cars, there is also a fuel return pipe that ensures that any excess fuel fed to the engine is safely returned to the tank. It also helps keep the fuel cool.

Another pipe connects the fuel vapour canister with the fuel tank, bringing back fuel that has evaporated.

Fuel filter
A fuel filter is located in the fuel pipe, at a point before the fuel enters the distribution device. Although most cars will have a coarse fuel filter inside the fuel tank, this is not enough.

A typical fuel filter has a paper-based mesh or thin layers of porous

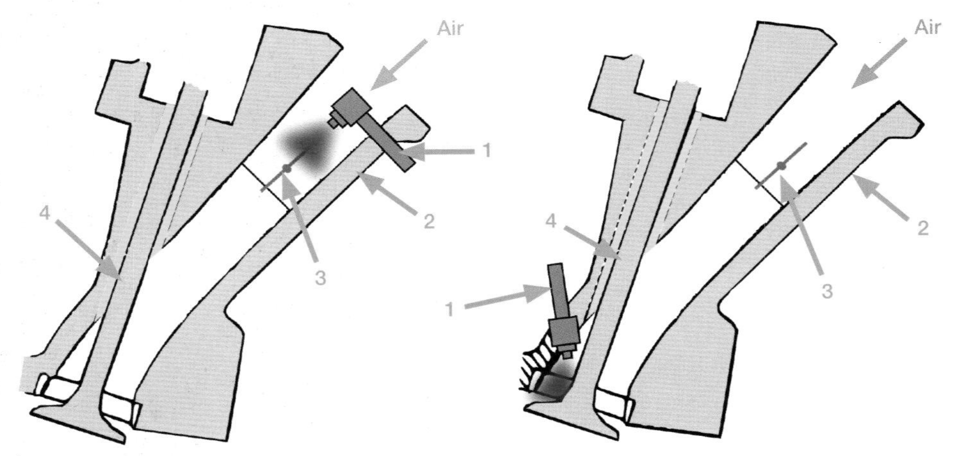

Fig 37: Fuel injector positions in a petrol/gasoline engine. Left: injector before butterfly. Right: injector behind butterfly. 1 Fuel injector, 2 ,throttle body, 3, throttle butterfly valve (open), 4 intake valve.

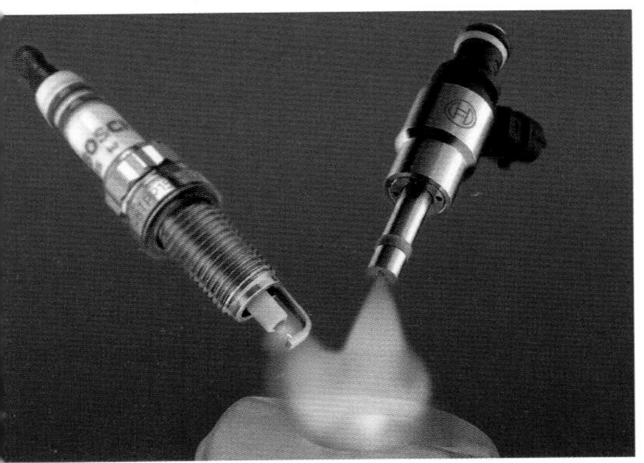

Fig 38: Direct injection system on a petrol/gasoline engine. Both the sparkplug and injector nozzle poke directly into the combustion chamber of a cylinder. (Courtesy Bosch)

metal to catch any sediment or dirt suspended in the fuel. Don't forget to regularly change the fuel filter in accordance with the car manufacturer's instructions.

Fuel injection system

The majority of today's four-stroke petrol (gasoline) engines use an 'indirect' injection system, where the injector squirts fuel into the intake manifold.

A throttle body injection system will deliver fuel ahead of the butterfly valve of the throttle body. While the so-called 'multiport' injection system will inject after the throttle body butterfly and close to an individual intake valve (see Fig 37).

Direct injection systems, where fuel is delivered straight into the individual combustion chamber of the cylinder, are usually associated with diesel engines. However, recently, high-pressure direct injection devices have been created for petrol engines – for example, almost every car made by Alfa Romeo now has a direct injection engine (see Fig 38).

Another non-diesel engine that can feature a high-pressure direct injection system is found in the new generation bi-fuel vehicles. Petrol (gasoline) is injected via a traditional multiport system, but the ethanol squirts straight into the combustion chamber through a direct injection system. Hooked up with a powerful computer control unit, there's plenty of potential in such engines.

The distribution device of a fuel injection system consists of a fuel rail (tubular chamber), a pressure regulator, and a set of injectors. The pressure regulator controls the fuel pressure in the rail by allowing fuel to return to the tank when the required pressure is reached. Connected to the fuel rail, the injectors have the intricate job of delivering fuel to the engine in just the right doses.

A fuel injector is an electro-mechanical needle valve. When there is a magnetic field in its wire windings the needle is pulled upwards, opening the orifice of the nozzle. When open, the fuel will squirt out as it is under constant pressure. The length of time the nozzle stays open (the longer it stays open, the richer – more fuel content – the combustible mixture will be), and the frequency with which it opens and closes, is determined by a computerised control system that collects information from a wide range of sensors.

There are eight main groups of sensors that provide the injection control system with data:

Lambda sensor – Fig 39. This measures the oxygen level in the engine's exhaust gases to determine whether the combustion is efficient. If the oxygen sensor says there's too much oxygen in the exhaust gases, the control unit understands that the combustible mixture isn't fully burning, and it will adjust the amount of fuel fed into the intake manifold accordingly.

Intake air temperature sensor – This provides a surefire way to safeguard against variable air density. Cool air is denser than warm air. Cold winter air will have more oxygen molecules, requiring more petrol molecules to burn efficiently.

Fig 39: Lamda (oxygen) sensor in the exhaust manifold (beneath the heatshield) of a Citröen C3.

Manifold pressure sensor – This measures the air pressure inside the intake manifold. High pressure inside the manifold is a sign of a high engine load, which consequently demands a richer mixture.

Coolant temperature sensor – While the engine is still cool, it needs a richer combustible mixture to warm it up quickly to the optimum operating temperature. Hence, when the coolant sensor thinks the engine is too cold, it will request that the control unit enrich the mixture.

Crankshaft speed sensor – This calculates the engine speed and allows the control unit to adjust injection timing.

Throttle opening sensor – One of the most important sensors that supplies data to the control unit. When the accelerator pedal is pushed, the sensors send a signal to the control unit saying 'we need more power.'

Knock sensor – This detects whether the combustible mixture is ignited at exactly the right time. Caused by a combination of heat and pressure, spontaneous combustion can occur at the wrong time. If this happens, a distinctive metallic knock can be heard. Knocks are very bad for the engine, and can be eliminated by adjusting the richness of the combustible mixture and fuel injection timing. On some turbocharged cars, the knock sensor also provides data to help adjust the turbo flow.

Airflow sensor – This calculates the volume of air flowing through the intake manifold. If the airflow increases, the sensor will send a signal to increase the amount of fuel provided, to match it to the volume of air.

Having considered all the incoming signals from the sensors, the computer control unit then determines the optimum working mode and sends out electronic impulses to the injectors. Each impulse opens a particular needle valve at a particular time and for a particular length of time, allowing fuel to be injected into the intake manifold.

A fuel injection system strives to achieve 'stoichiometry.' Yes, that sounds really clever! What it actually means is the perfect balance between the number of petrol molecules and oxygen molecules needed to make the combustible mixture at any given moment, so that no excess molecules are left in the combustion chamber after the explosion. An engine working in a stoichiometrical balance would indeed be very efficient, but in the real world we can only strive to achieve this, and modern injection control systems get us ever closer.

Engine idle speed control system (petrol/gasoline engines)

When you start the car, when you stop at the traffic lights, or when you disengage the clutch to change the gears, the engine works in the idle mode. It keeps working at low revs and gets only enough fuel to avoid stalling. It will also have to sustain all the ancillary systems, like the water pump and air-conditioning, during the idling period. The engine idle speed control system takes care of this, otherwise you'd need to restart the engine each time you released the accelerator pedal.

Fig 40. The idle speed is sustained by a simple bypass channel in the throttle body. When you release the accelerator the butterfly valve in the throttle body closes, but the bypass remains open and delivers the air volume necessary to sustain the lowest

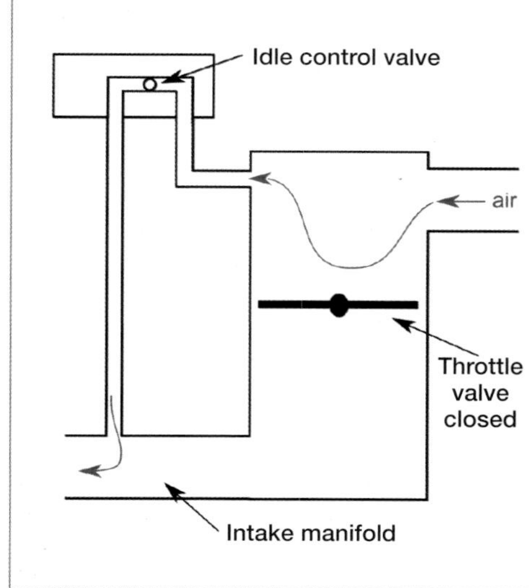

Fig 40: Idle speed controller mechanism.

sensible idle speed (it is usually just below 1000rpm for petrol engines, and around 700rpm for diesels).

On modern vehicles the size of the bypass is adjusted by the electronic control unit. There is also a thermo valve which senses the temperature of incoming air and which will further increase the idle airflow when the engine is cold.

Fig 41: Typical air intake system. 1 Air intake duct, 2 Air filter casing, 3 Duct to intake manifold.

Air intake system

Fig 41. The air intake system starts with a plastic nozzle that sucks air into the air cleaner chamber, which contains a renewable air filter. Having passed through the air cleaner air flows through an air duct and through the throttle body (petrol/gasoline engines only) before entering the intake manifold.

Fig 42. A throttle body is a small device that connects the air duct with the intake manifold of the engine. It controls the volume of air flowing into the intake manifold in response to the accelerator pedal. The butterfly-type valve (a disc pivoting on a central spindle) inside the throttle bod (gas) pedal through a series of wires, or by tiny electric motors, which take the information from the car's electronic control unit. Modern engines can have a separate throttle body for each cylinder.

Air filters should be renewed on a regular basis in accordance with the vehicle manufacturer's instructions. Driving with a clean air filter will ensure the longevity of the engine and the maximum available power.

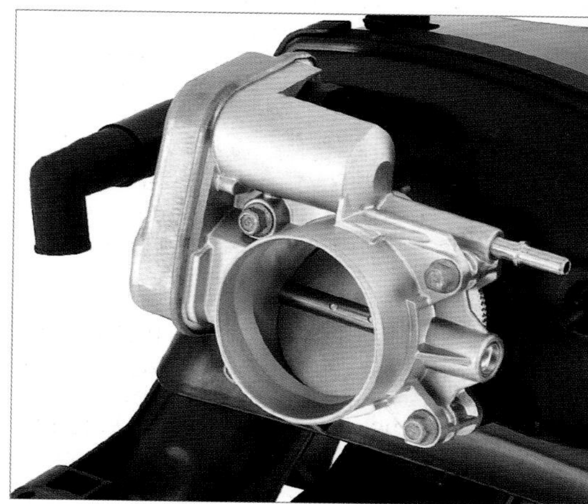
Fig 42: Throttle body. This one is electronically controlled – not directly by a cable from accelerator pedal. The gold-coloured disc on a spindle is the throttle butterfly which controls the amount of air entering the manifold. (Courtesy General Motors)

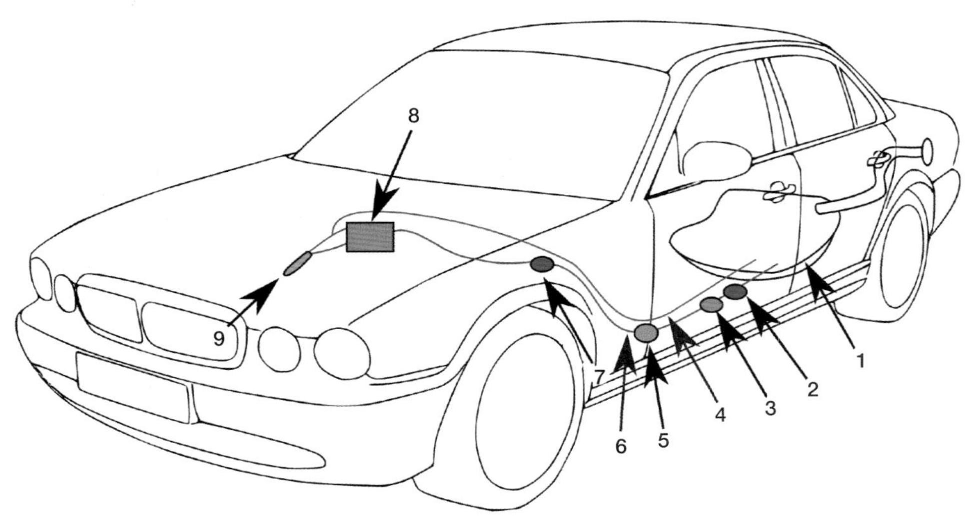

Fig 43: Fuel system of a diesel car. 1 Fuel tank, 2 Low pressure supply pump, 3 Water-fuel separator, 4 Fuel return line, 5 Fuel heater, 6 Fuel line, 7 Fuel filter, 8 High pressure pump, 9 Fuel injectors.

Fuel system of a diesel engine

Just like the fuel system of a petrol engine, the diesel will have a fuel tank, in-tank pump/pick-up, fuel filter, and a distribution system at the engine. Here the similarities end. In fact, the diesel fuel system is very different.

The main peculiarity is that a diesel car has no throttle. You simply cannot control the airflow. Instead the engine output is controlled by the injection pump, which adjusts the amount of fuel that is fed into each cylinder.

On the compression stroke of a petrol (gasoline) engine, the piston travels upwards compressing the fuel air mix sucked in on the last downward stroke. However, on the compression stroke of a diesel engine the piston travels upwards with only clean air

Fig 44: A modern diesel distribution pump. (Courtesy Bosch)

above it, and when it reaches the top, the compressed air gets very hot and ignites the diesel fuel that is puffed into the combustion chamber at that very moment. So you see, controlling the air volume wouldn't make any sense, because in a diesel, you always want the cylinder full of air, no matter what, otherwise we wouldn't get the optimum compression.

Compression is the key in diesel engines. Compared to petrol/gasoline engines with compression ratios of 8:1 to 10:1, the compression ratio of a diesel engine is 14:1 to 25:1. Compression ratio is a quotient between the volume of a cylinder's combustion chamber and the cylinder itself above the piston crown when the piston is at its lowest point (called BDC – bottom dead centre) and the volume when the piston is at the top of its stroke (called TDC – top dead centre). For example if we take the 14:1 compression ratio it means that the volume of air in the cylinder/combustion chamber at TDC is squeezed into one fourteenth of the space that it occupied at BDC.

In order to inject fuel, diesel fuel pumps must provide extremely high pressure, otherwise, considering that there is already very high pressure inside the cylinder, the injector would fail to squirt in the fuel.

The basic diesel injection system consists of injection pump, injection lines, injectors, and glow plugs.

The injection pump is what controls the amount of fuel fed to each injector. It also provides precise timing for each injection. Normally, the fuel system is powered by an in-line diesel injection pump. A separate plunger (small piston) is dedicated to each cylinder. The plungers are operated by a camshaft driven by the engine. The pump camshaft looks similar to the camshaft that operates the engine valve train. It too has lobes pushing the plungers up and down as it rotates once for every two revolutions of the crankshaft. Each time a lobe pushes a plunger, highly pressurised fuel is driven out of the plunger, into the injection line, and out of the injector. The amount of fuel delivered is controlled by a rack and pinion mechanism. The more you push the accelerator pedal, the further the rack will go, aligning the plunger so that it delivers more fuel.

Considering that each cylinder wants to receive the same amount of fuel, an even simpler solution is a distribution injection pump. Unlike the in-line pump, this one has only one plunger, which distributes the same amount of fuel to each injection line. A distribution injection pump can provide a simpler solution from the manufacturer's point of view, as it won't need the sophisticated rack and pinion mechanism. The amount of fuel delivered is controlled by a lever connecting the accelerator pedal to the pump.

Unlike the petrol injector, which is an electromagnetic valve, the diesel fuel injector (in the case of both an in-line pump and distribution injection pump) is a mechanical valve. It will open the needle when it succumbs to the incoming fuel pressure (that is each time the pump plunger sends highly pressurised fuel into the injector). When sufficient pressure is felt, the needle pops up, allowing a precise dosage of fuel to squirt into the cylinder. Depending on the nozzle configuration the fuel spray will be either a nice cone-shaped mist of fuel, or a cylindrical one. Some manufacturers choose to have multi-hole nozzles because they believe improves the combustion, as fuel comes out of different points simultaneously.

Common rail injection

Figs 45 & 46. Mechanical injection is absolutely fine – its been around for decades and can achieve really precise fuel distribution. However, many diesel cars made after 2005 will feature a common rail diesel injection system, which is, in fact, very different from the two systems described earlier. The main downside of a mechanical fuel distribution system is that the fuel pump speed is proportional to engine speed, which means that injection pressure is related to engine speed too. As a result, the injection system works best when the engine speed is reasonably high. Efficient burning cannot be achieved

Fig 45: A modern diesel engine with a common fuel rail (1) and direct injection (2) to the combustion chambers. (Courtesy Mazda)

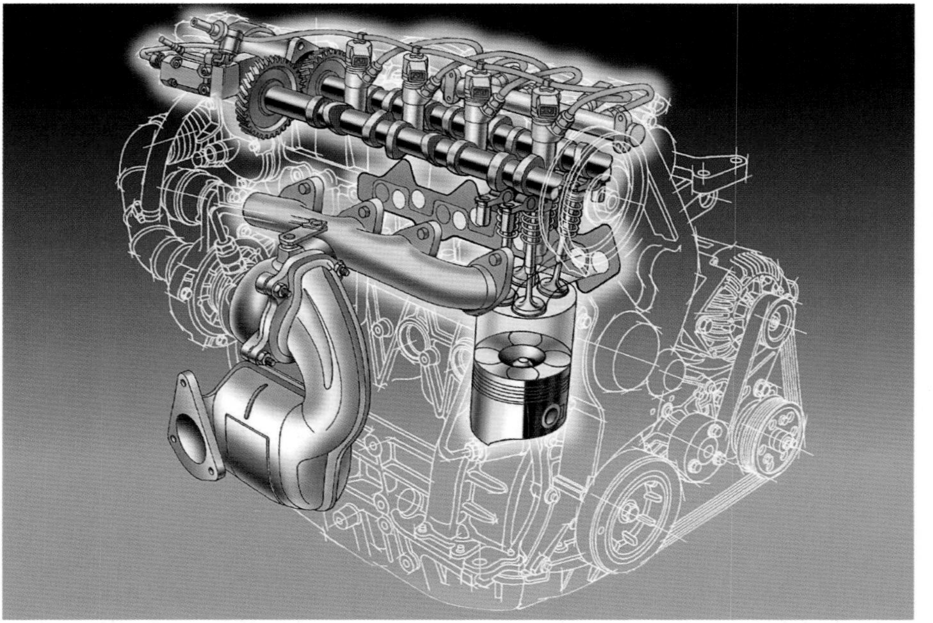

Fig 46: Schematic of a common rail fuel system which delivers high-pressure fuel to individual injectors. Green: High pressure-pump, Yellow: Common fuel rail, fuel lines and injectors, Violet: Intake manifold, Blue: Cylinder, piston and valvetrain. (Courtesy Renault)

when the engine is on low revs. Common rail systems have resolved this issue completely.

The term 'common rail' refers to a reservoir of highly-pressurised fuel serving all the injectors. Thus, the fuel pump has to produce pressure only in the common rail rather than at each separate injector.

Common rail systems are controlled by an engine/electronic control unit (ECU), therefore, they can achieve even better fuel distribution compared to mechanical pumps. In reality, you can have constant fuel pressure inside the common rail regardless of engine speed. Diesel injectors on a common rail system are driven by an electromagnetic valve. When the control unit recognises that it's time to inject, it releases the valve, and the high fuel pressure pushes the needle up. Once sufficient fuel has been injected, the control unit closes the electromagnetic valve.

As electronics are involved, a common rail system can perform several injections per stroke. The main injection is sometimes preceded by a pre-injection or a pilot injection to achieve smoother combustion.

Apart from having a direct influence on the injectors, the ECU will also control the pressure regulation valve so that there's always the right pressure inside the rail. And we are talking about really high pressures here: inside a modern common rail system it can easily reach 2068bar/30,000psi.

The ECU makes its decisions according to the data provided by various sensors, which supply it with a continuous stream of information. The main sensors are: fuel temperature sensor; common rail pressure sensor; reference mark; crankshaft speed sensor; accelerator pedal position sensor; load pressure sensor; and air temperature sensor.

Glow plugs

Diesel engines rely on appropriate temperatures (common rail systems to a lesser extent) to carry out successful combustion. That's why, compared to a petrol (gasoline) engine, it is more difficult to start a cold diesel. However, providing the battery and starter motor are functioning efficiently, you should be able to start a diesel even at very low temperatures. To make life easier, each cylinder has a small glow plug that begins heating the air in the pre-combustion chamber when you turn the ignition key to the appropriate position.

Engine idle speed control system

As there is no throttle and no bypass to maintain the idle speed of a diesel engine, the idle control function is carried out by the diesel injection pump. Even when your foot is not on the accelerator pedal, the plungers will receive a small amount of fuel to keep the engine running.

Ignition system

Fig 47. The purpose of the ignition system in a petrol/gasoline engine is to create a spark to ignite the combustible mixture in the combustion chamber. Unfortunately, the voltage in the car battery is too low to produce a spark hot enough to perform this function. Some sort of transformer is needed. The ignition coil is a step-up transformer that changes the input 12 volts into 30,000 volts at output – more than enough to create a nice big spark.

The high voltage charge can now be transmitted to a sparkplug that sits with its tip poking into the combustion chamber. There are two electrodes at its tip separated by a small gap, and when a high voltage is applied to the sparkplug the current jumps between

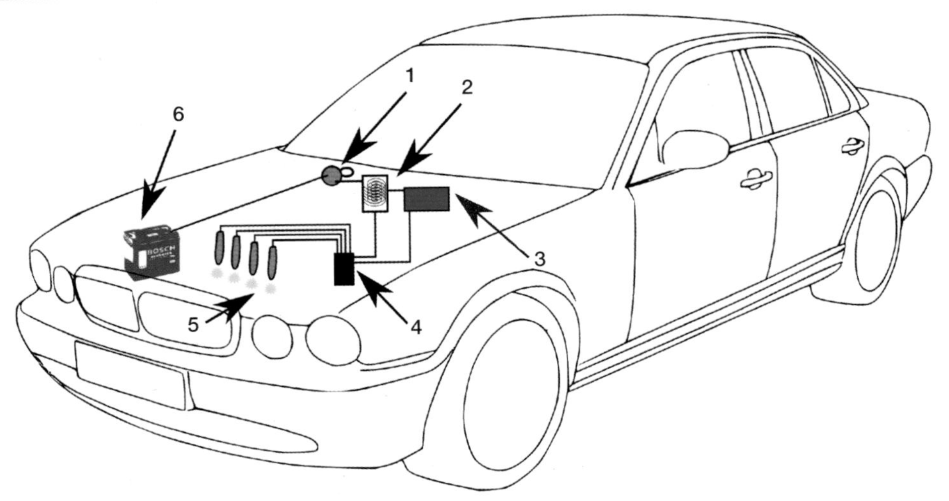

Fig 47: Ignition system. 1 Ignition key (or button) 2 Ignition coil (there might be one for each spark plug), 3 Control unit, 4 Distributor, 5 Sparkplugs, 6 Battery.

the electrodes. However, as there are multiple cylinders and the spark is needed in each only at certain points in time, a distribution system is used. It will determine which sparkplug will get the charge, and when.

Modern engines use a distribution system that is operated according to exact measurements of engine speed. By placing position sensors on the crankshaft or flywheel, it is possible to measure the precise position of every piston and to use the data to optimise spark timing very precisely. The crankshaft position is transmitted to the car's ECU (engine/electronic control unit), which sends signals to the distributor so that it sends the high-voltage charge exactly when needed for each cylinder.

A more advanced system is the distributorless ignition system. A magnetic trigger wheel is mounted on the crankshaft. It interacts with the crankshaft position sensor, and sends signals to the ECU so that it can determine which sparkplug to fire, and exactly when. The distributorless system still uses a centralised ignition coil.

Even more advanced, direct ignition systems are now in use which have a trigger wheel just like distributorless systems. The difference is that the centralised ignition coil has gone. Now each sparkplug has its own dedicated coil attached to it, and each coil receives a signal from the computer to tell it when to fire.

As for diesel fans, I've got some good news for you. There's no ignition system on a diesel car simply because it doesn't need one. A diesel engine ignites the fuel mixture using the super-heated compressed air inside the cylinders. That's why the majority of military vehicles are diesel – you can waterproof a diesel engine quite easily, whereas driving a petrol (gasoline) car through deep water can be a nightmare, mainly because of the electric ignition system.

Cooling system

Fig 48. It's well-known that internal combustion engines are really hot-headed. The moment the combustible mixture explodes, the internal temperature of the combustion chamber is around 2000°C/3632°F.

Exposed to such extreme temperatures, if left uncontrolled, the engine would soon melt – the melting point for iron is 1500°C/2732°F and for aluminium as low as 650°C/689°F. Luckily, the temperature spikes last for a very short time, and there is a cooling system to take the excess heat away.

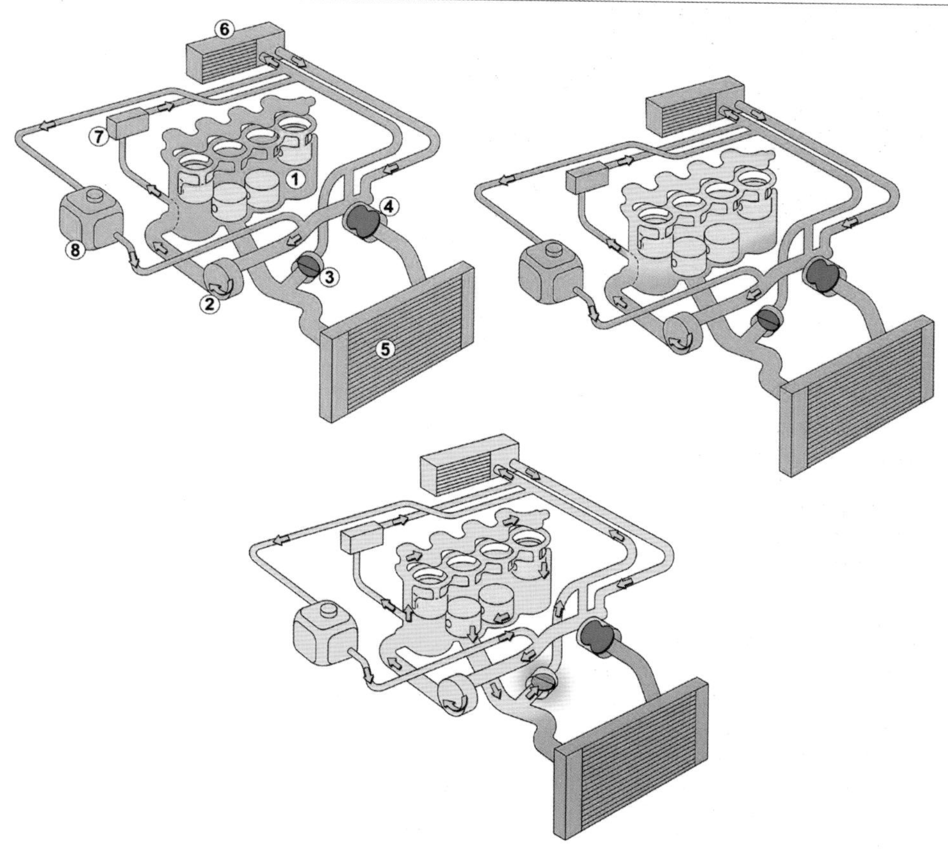

Fig 48: Temperature management in a liquid-cooled engine. 1 Engine, 2 Water pump, 3 Flow valve, 4 Thermostat, 5 Radiator, 6 Air heater for the interior, 7 Exhaust gas recirculation cooler, 8 Expansion/top-up reservoir. The first schematic shows a cold engine – the valve closes and restricts coolant circulation around the cylinders, so that they can heat up faster. The second schematic shows how the cylinders are getting warm. The third schematic shows how the valve opens once the engine has reached a certain temperature. At this point the thermostat valve should open and the cooling, via the radiator, can begin. (Courtesy Renault)

The cooling system is very intricate – it needs to maintain a perfect temperature balance. The engine shouldn't be allowed to overheat, nor should it be kept too cool. The normal working temperature of the engine is just below 100ºC/212ºF and, until the temperature reaches some 80ºC/176ºF, its operation will be very inefficient. A cool engine has too wide a clearance between the pistons and the cylinder walls, the combustible mixture burns inefficiently, and the oil is too cold and thick to provide proper lubrication. So, the quicker the engine reaches its optimum temperature, the better.

The most basic engine cooling system is air cooling, in which no liquid circulates around the engine – it relies solely on ambient air flowing over cooling fins to maintain optimum temperature. As no air-cooled cars are produced today, we will spend no more time on this subject.

All modern engines are water-cooled. However, actually, water is only one part of the coolant liquid. Unless the manufacturer has specified otherwise, your car coolant consists of one part distilled water and one part antifreeze. The latter is added to ensure the coolant doesn't freeze during cold spells, and it also possesses some anti-corrosion properties (particularly important for engines with aluminium cylinder heads and/or cylinder blocks).

The coolant liquid circulates around the cylinders, cylinder head and, often, the intake manifold, through various internal waterways cast into these components. The liquid coolant is driven around the cylinder block and cylinder head by a water pump, which is powered by a drivebelt from a pulley on the front of the crankshaft. The water pump ensures the liquid travels through the engine, and into the cabin heater, then back to the radiator, where it is cooled by passing air which is helped to flow through the radiator, when needed, by a huge fan.

The cooling system is very important. Only about half of the heat generated by the engine is driven away through the exhaust system, and a further ten per cent is absorbed by the lubrication system. Dispersal of the remainder is the responsibility of the cooling system. A water pump has to cope with an immense task – under normal driving conditions it drives all of the liquid through the engine block, cylinder head, intake manifold, water hoses and radiator every nine seconds.

Most water pumps are centrifugal, creating pressure difference and pumping water via an impeller, which sounds similar to a propeller, but is different. A propeller propels fluid along its axis of rotation; an impeller throws the fluid from its centre towards its edges. As the impeller is encased inside a housing, the liquid has no other option but to move forward. The engine fan, on the other hand, is a propeller – it moves particles (the air) from the front towards the back of its blades.

Moving water is a hard job, and there's plenty of it. Coolant capacity – depending on engine size – is usually between 8 and 13 litres/1.76 and 2.85 Imp. gallons/2.11 and 3.43 US gallons. In order to move that amount of water in just 9 seconds, the pump has to consume a great deal of power and, as it is driven by the crankshaft, it can contribute to excessive fuel consumption. Although the majority of impellers are made of metal, some newer models are made of sturdy plastic. The impeller fins are another area for the modern car engineers to improve – straight fins consume less engine power, but aren't as efficient.

The radiator is connected to the engine via two large 'rubber' hoses.

A flexible material is used to withstand the vibrations of the engine. The upper hose ('top hose') is the inlet, and the lower one ('bottom hose' is the outlet. So that the airflow can efficiently cool it, the coolant has to flow from the top of the radiator to the bottom, or alternatively from one side to the other. The radiator comprises tanks at top and bottom connected together by many small tubes between fin walls which provide a large total surface area, so that the air flowing through it can take away as much heat as possible.

The upper hose usually comes into the radiator from the thermostat housing. The thermostat controls the coolant flow by detecting the temperature and acting accordingly. While the engine is still cool, the thermostat ensures the water is driven through a bypass, so that no cold water flows through the engine. Once the engine nears its optimum operational temperature, the thermostat opens a valve and lets the coolant flow through the whole system. The lower hose from the radiator feeds the cool water back into the water pump, which distributes the liquid through the engine's waterways. A coolant reservoir is connected to the radiator. Its main purpose is to show the level of coolant liquid and to provide an easily accessible point for topping up.

It is very important to check the coolant level at least once a week. If it's below the top level mark, top it up with equal parts distilled water and antifreeze. If the coolant level drops regularly, more serious maintenance or repair is necessary. Low coolant level can indicate leaks in water hoses, the radiator, heater or water pump: even more seriously a damaged head gasket (the seal between the engine block and cylinder head). Remember to check the coolant when the engine is cool, and never open the reservoir on a hot engine. The escaping steam can cause serious injuries.

The whole volume of coolant should be drained and changed every two years even if no leakages are detected.

Lubrication system

Fig 49. The lubrication system distributes engine oil to critical friction points around the engine. Oil creates a sort of a safety cushion between the surfaces of moving parts. As a secondary function, the lubrication system also assists in cooling the engine. Without proper lubrication, even with the cooling system in place, the engine would seize in a matter of minutes. The temperatures caused by friction would melt bearings and cause terrible damage.

The engine oil is held in a sump (oil pan) at the base of the engine. Oil is drawn from the sump through a pick-up device into the oil pump, which drives it through an oil filter and into the engine and turbocharger (if you car has one).

An alternative is a 'dry sump' configuration. It is often used on high-performance sports cars to avoid the oil starvation problems caused by oil surging around in the sump. A dry sump employs external oil reservoirs and collection pumps, which ensure that oil is delivered to the engine whatever its angle or the centrifugal forces caused by fast cornering. You are unlikely to find a dry sump on a family car, but everyone considering serious off-roading should think about converting their 4x4s to a dry sump configuration. Otherwise when you tackle a really steep hill, the engine could be starved of oil.

Oil travels to the vital parts of the engine though oil passages. The parts in direct contact with each other

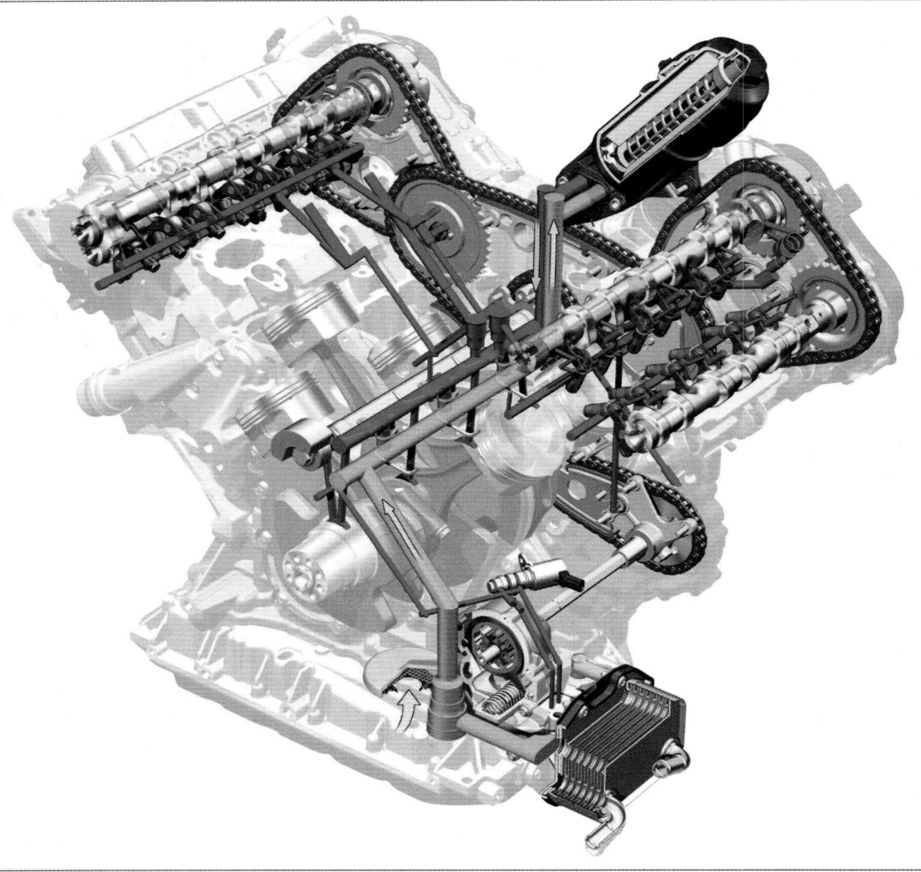

Fig 49: Lubrication system. Red: Heated oil enters radiator (not all cars will have an oil radiator), Yellow: Oil flows to the oil filter, Green: Oil is distributed to the vital parts of the engine through oilways. (Courtesy Audi)

(for example, a shaft and its bearing) have a tiny clearance (usually around 0.05mm/0.0020in) to allow the oil to seep in and form a protective film. The oil pump delivers oil to the crankshaft bearings, camshaft bearings, valvetrain and, if fitted, turbocharger. The bottom part of the engine is oiled by the flow that returns from the top parts.

It's important to check the oil level in the sump once a week. You should check the engine oil level engine at least five minutes after it's been switched off as otherwise you'll get a false reading. The car must be on level ground. Remove the dipstick, wipe its tip with a paper tissue, and then re-insert it. Remove it again, paying attention to the marks on its tip. It usually has two: 'Full' and 'Refill.' If the level is low, add some oil through the oil filler cap, but be careful not to overfill.

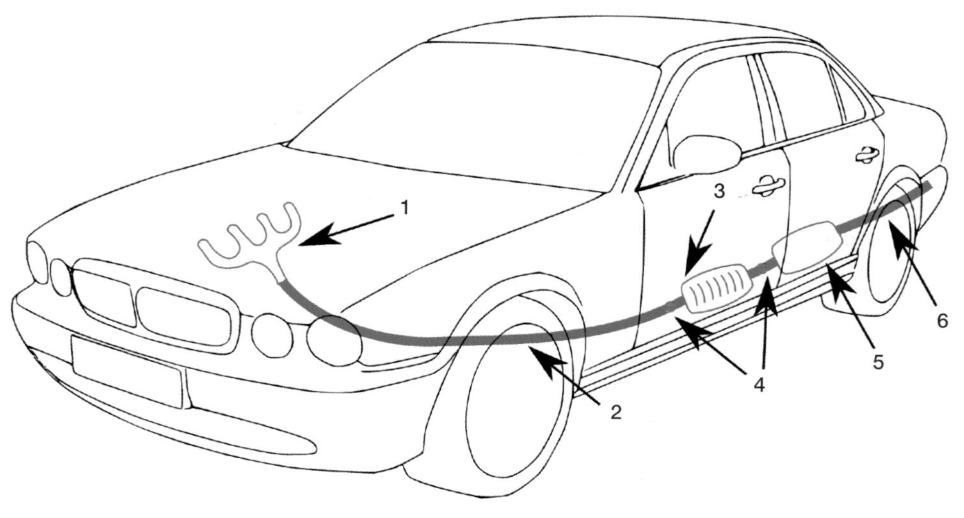

Fig 50: Exhaust system. 1 Exhaust manifold, 2 Exhaust pipe, 3 Catalytic converter, 4 Lamda (oxygen sensors) the first may be in the exhaust manifold much closer to the engine, 5 Silencer/ Muffler, 6 Tailpipe.

Be aware that the dipstick tip is a very crude measure. There are between 4 and 8 litres/0.88 and 1.76 Imp. gallons/1.06 and 2.11 US gallons of oil in the sump. If the dipstick level falls by one eighth, don't assume that one eighth of the oil has been lost. Adding just half a litre/one pint may cause overfill, so experiment with very small amounts at first.

Engine oil should be changed religiously according to the car manufacturers schedule, more often if you like. The oil filter should be changed with every oil change.

Exhaust system

Fig 50. The main purpose of the engine's exhaust system is to get rid of the gaseous by-products of combustion. It also takes a part in cooling the engine. As you may already know, almost 50 per cent of waste heat produced by the engine leaves through the exhaust system.

Its main components are the exhaust manifold, exhaust pipes, catalytic converter, silencer (muffler), and tailpipe. A modern exhaust system also sustains the environment by providing the means to capture and convert some of the dangerous substances that would otherwise escape.

An engine exhaust system is driven by exhaust gas pressure. When the exhaust valve is open, the piston pushes the gases into the exhaust manifold and further down the pipes. No external source of extraction is necessary. The art of designing modern exhaust systems revolves around lowering the amount of baddies coming out of the tailpipe.

An older car with a 4-cylinder

engine can have the CO_2 emission level as high as 500g/km, mainly due to improper combustion and a weak exhaust system. An ultra-modern car with a similar engine will only emit around 150g/km of CO_2.

Although CO_2 emissions are the favourite topic for people involved in the ongoing climate change debate, there are many more harmful substances coming out of the tailpipe that aren't receiving the attention they really deserve. In the 1990s only around 60 per cent of car-related air pollution was directly caused by engine exhaust gases. The remainder was caused by unwanted fuel evaporation. Today the engineers have managed to solve many of the evaporation-related problems.

Apart from the obvious by-product of burned fuel – the CO_2 – there are four main groups of unwanted substances escaping into the atmosphere ...

Solid particles – small bits of soot mainly caused by the additives mixed into fuel. A diesel engine with a bungled fuel distribution (when too much fuel is fed into the cylinder) can produce soot without any additives. Part of the soot is heavy enough to end up on road surfaces and be washed away into the drainage system. The remainder – and that's what we are really worried about – is made up from tiny particles that become airborne and travel unbelievable distances without ever landing.

Hydrocarbons – caused by unburned fuel escaping through the exhaust. Another source of hydrocarbons is vapours from the fuel system.

Nitrous oxides – part of the exhaust gases due to the fact that air is made of 79 per cent of nitrogen. The higher the combustion heat inside the cylinder, the more likely it is that nitrogen will form a bond with oxygen. In fact, a richer combustible mixture would produce significantly less nitrous oxide; on the other hand, increasing the fuel content in the combustible mixture would cause the hydrocarbon emission levels to soar. What we really want is a balance. An engine operating in a stoichometrical balance wouldn't produce any nitrous oxide at all, because the oxygen would have reacted with the fuel to the last molecule. Unfortunately, stoichometrical engines exist only in the ideal world.

Carbon monoxide emissions – caused by partly burned fuel. A leaner combustible mixture would produce only a very small amount of carbon monoxide. Still, it would also increase the amount of nitrous oxides produced.

When all of the engineering efforts to make combustion super efficient have been exhausted, we're left with the daunting task of capturing as many of the unwanted substances as possible. A modern computerised emission control system can do a great job.

Catalytic converter

Fig 51. A catalytic converter is one of the simplest and most important tools in battling hydrocarbons and carbon monoxide emissions. Its operation is based on burning the emissions at high temperatures to convert them into non-toxic CO_2 and water vapour. Usually 600-700°C/1112-1292°F is enough to get the hydrocarbons burning – however, the problem is the size of the converter. The amount of time the exhaust gases spend inside the converter is strictly limited, which is why the designers had to come up with a special solution. And they did by introducing a catalyst. From chemistry lessons you may remember that a catalyst is a substance that speeds up a chemical reaction by being present during the reaction, but not actually taking part in it. For carbon compounds,

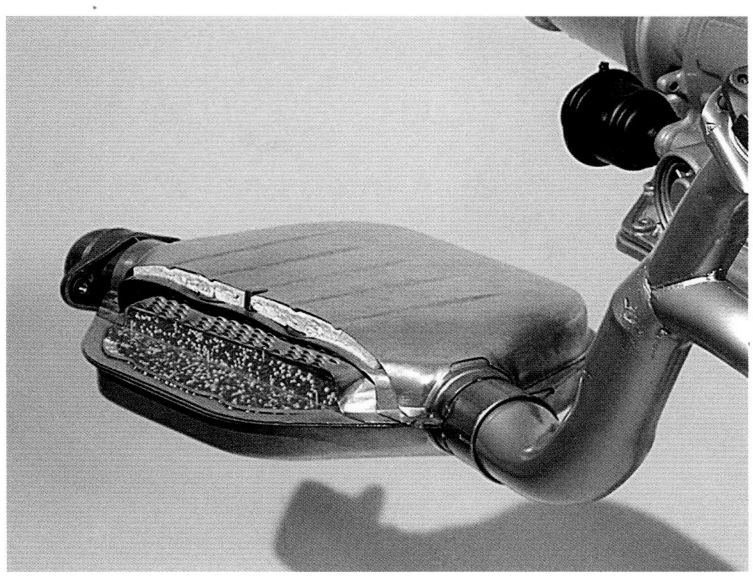

Fig 51: A look inside a catalytic converter. (Courtesy General Motors)

the ideal catalyst is a mix of noble metals like platinum and palladium. They are extremely expensive, which is why the bulk of a converter is made of ceramic material covered in a thin layer of catalyst. More up-to-date converters will also have rhodium as an additional catalyst to enable them to burn nitrous oxides.

The converter doesn't need any additional power from outside; it heats itself with the hot exhaust gases, and thus is normally very efficient.

There are three main types of catalytic converters: two-way, three-way, and dual-bed. A two-way converter can only deal with hydrocarbons and carbon monoxide. A three-way model will deal with the former, plus nitrous oxides. The latest cars have a dual-bed converter installed. The first chamber is a three-way catalyst dealing with all three main offenders. The second one is a two-way converter finishing off the excess hydrocarbons and carbon monoxide. Between the chambers there is an air inlet used by an air pump to drive more oxygen into the converter, improving the burning process.

Positive crankcase ventilation system

Fig 52. A positive crankcase ventilation system is one of the many ways to recapture the unburned fuel. Certain amount of combustible mixture will leak past the piston rings and down into the crankcase, even if the engine is in excellent condition. Gases ending up in the crankcase are called 'blowby.'

Modern cars have a positive crankcase ventilation system (PVC). Positive – not because they're doing good job but because the system is powered by the engine's own vacuum.

The PVC consists of a hose and a valve joining the crankcase with the intake manifold. The idea is to push the blowby back into the cylinders so that it burns properly. The valve is there to control the flow from the crankcase to the intake manifold. For example,

Fig 52: The shiny black pipe (the one that looks like a shower hose: arrowed) is the main part of the exhaust gas recirculation system. (Courtesy BMW)

the valve will stop ventilation when the engine is idling so that it can sustain the optimum idle speed.

Blowby can cause corrosion of the bottom end of the engine, and also spoils the engine oil. So, the PVC system also takes part in engine maintenance. A clever little system!

Gas recirculation and air pumps

To further reduce the toxic emissions there are some additional intricate devices installed on modern engines. The exhaust gas recirculation system directs a portion of exhaust gases back into the intake manifold to reduce the amount of nitrous oxide, by inhibiting the peak temperatures of combustion. The volume of exhaust gases fed back to the intake manifold is regulated by a gas recirculation valve.

An air pump can be installed to drive fresh oxygen into the catalytic converter, or in some cases directly into the exhaust manifold. The exhaust gases escaping the cylinders are so hot that if you provide fresh oxygen to them they will continue burning. And that's what we really want – for the fuel to burn completely before the gases are pushed out into the atmosphere. Adding an air pump will significantly reduce the hydrocarbon and carbon monoxide contents in the exhaust gases.

Unfortunately, just like the PVC system, both the gas recirculation system and air pump reduce the power of the engine, the latter largely due to the fact that the air pump is driven by the crankshaft.

Lambda (oxygen) sensor

Fig 53. The emissions on a modern vehicle are often controlled by a computer. Usually it is the same unit that

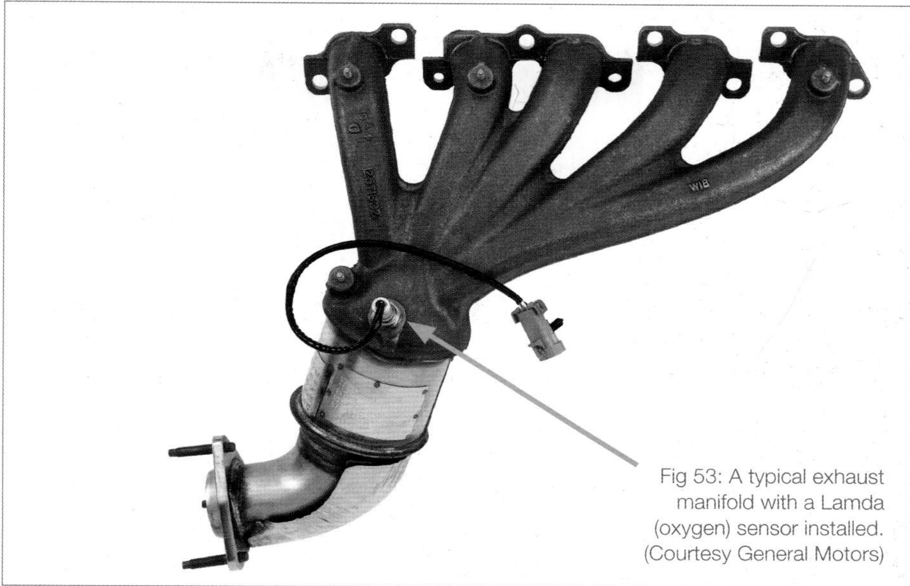

Fig 53: A typical exhaust manifold with a Lamda (oxygen) sensor installed. (Courtesy General Motors)

controls the ignition and fuel system. As you may remember, it receives data from a large amount of various sensors. When it comes to emission controls, the most important one is the oxygen sensor. Volvo fans will recognize it as a 'lambda sond.'

The lambda sensor measures the oxygen content in the engine's exhaust gasses. Its main function is to help adjust the fuel/air mix fed to the combustion chambers by determining whether the fuel is being burned efficiently. Excess oxygen in the exhaust gases means that the combustible mixture hasn't fully burned. A signal is then sent back to the control unit, which will adjust the amount of fuel in the fuel/ air mix.

On modern vehicles it is not unusual to find more than one lambda sensor. By monitoring the exhaust in more than one place the ECU gets the bigger picture. The first lambda sensor is usually located in the exhaust manifold, before the catalytic converter. The data it gathers is used to adjust the fuel mixture. The second sensor is located after the catalytic converter to determine whether the maximum amount of toxic substances is being burned. The data provided by the second lambda sensor is used to control the oxygen fed into the catalytic converter.

The lambda sensor's operation is based on the difference in oxygen content between its inner cavity and outer surface. The inner cavity is exposed to the atmosphere, which means 21 per cent oxygen content. The outer surface comes into direct contact with the exhaust gases, which will have a very different oxygen content. Heated to high temperatures and helped by catalytic substances, the sensor will generate a voltage difference between its two surfaces, according to the percentage of oxygen in the exhaust gases. The voltage difference is relayed to the ECU.

three
Drivetrain

Clutch

The clutch is a mechanical device between the engine and manual gearbox (transmission) that allows the drive from the engine to be smoothly and progressively engaged and disengaged from the gearbox.

The clutch assembly comprises four major elements:

1) The smooth rear face of the flywheel.

2) The friction disc (a round disc with friction material on both sides),

3) The cover plate, which encloses another smooth-faced metal disc on the friction plate side.

4) The clutch release bearing.

The cover plate bolts to the flywheel, clamping the friction disc between it and the flywheel.

The friction disc has a hollow centre which is internally splined to engage with splines on the gearbox input shaft, along which it is free to slide. The clutch cover incorporates a diaphragm spring which controls the pressure with which the friction plate is clamped. The clutch release bearing has a hollow centre so that it can slide along the gearbox input shaft when the clutch pedal is operated in order to apply pressure to the centre fingers of the diaphragm spring. The tension applied by the pressure plate to squeeze the clutch friction disc between it and the flywheel face can be altered by the degree of pressure the clutch release bearing applies to the centre of the diaphragm spring.

Fig 54. When the clutch pedal is pressed, the release bearing pushes on the centre of the diaphragm spring causing a distortion in the spring which reduces the pressure applied to the friction disc at the spring's circumference, thus allowing it to slip between the flywheel and pressure plate faces. When the clutch pedal is fully depressed, the friction disk finds itself released completely from clamping

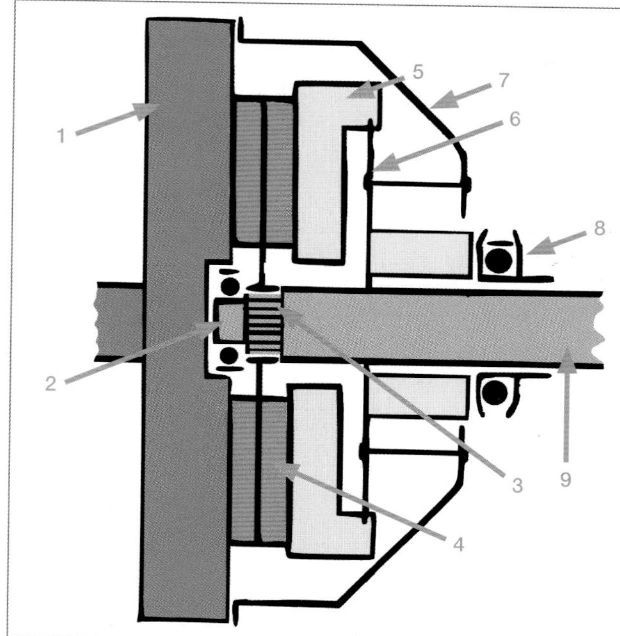

Fig 54: A simplified schematic of a clutch. 1 Flywheel, 2 Spigot bearing, 3 Splines, 4 Clutch friction disc, 5 Smooth-faced metal disc, 6 Diapraghm spring (would actually be a little dished), 7 Clutch cover (actuall bolted to flywheel), 8 Clutch release bearing, 9 Gearbox input (first motion) shaft.

pressure, and so no engine power is transmitted to the gearbox. As the clutch pedal is gradually released, the release bearing gradually reduces the pressure it applies to the diaphragm spring; this in turn gradually tightens the squeezing force applied to the friction disc until a point is reached, progressively, whereby the friction disc is tightly held – locked – between the flywheel and the pressure plate. By this mechanism engine power is transferred smoothly to the gearbox and, ultimately, to the car's driving wheels.

Gearbox (transmission unit)

The gearbox allows the ratio between the engine's speed (revs per minute) and the speed with which the driving wheels are turned to be altered in steps (or gears). It basically contains a set of gearwheels (you might call them cogs) that you can engage in different combinations to get the car to do what you want, and even to travel in reverse.

The two main types of gearbox (transmission unit) are manual and automatic.

Manual transmission

A simple principle is behind the operation of any car transmission. If a small gear drives a large gear, the large gear will turn slowly but will exert high torque (turning force). If a large gear turns a small gear, the small gear will turn much faster than the large gear, but will have little torque.

When first gear is selected, a small gear drives a larger one. The car will move relatively slowly in relation to the engine speed, but maximum torque is available. So, if you need the car to move off from a stationary position first gear makes the most sense as a lot of torque is required to overcome the inertia of the car's weight. As you progress through the gears, the driven wheels will turn faster and faster in relation to the engine speed, but the torque will reduce with each gear. That's why you cannot usually drive up a steep hill in fourth or fifth gear – there's simply not enough torque at the driven wheels to keep the car in motion. On the other hand, 4th and 5th gears are ideal for economical and efficient cruising because, once the car has reached a comfortable speed, it doesn't need as much torque at the driven wheels as when it started moving. Constantly choosing a higher gear as road speed increases will allow engine revs to be kept to a minimum, saving fuel and treating the engine kindly.

The speed difference between gears is called the 'gear ratio.' It represents the relationship between the number of revolutions a drive gear makes in order for the driven gear to make one full revolution. Here is a typical gear ratio sequence for a modern passenger car – 1st gear: 3.25:1 (this means that the engine crankshaft will make 3.25 revolutions for every single revolution of the transmission's output).

2nd gear: 1.78:1
3rd gear: 1.19:1
4th gear: 1:1
5th gear: 0.65:1
Reverse gear: 3:1.

Fig 55. A typical manual gearbox has four shafts that carry a set of gears each. The input shaft (or first motion shaft) is rotated by the engaged clutch. Beneath the input shaft is the countershaft (or layshaft) which carries several gearwheels. The output shaft is located on the same axis as the input shaft and, at first glance, it and the input shaft look like a single long shaft. However, when the gear lever is in neutral position, the input shaft will revolve while the output shaft does not. In operation the countershaft transfers power from the input shaft to the output shaft by engaging different gear combinations with the counter shaft. There is an additional, smaller shaft called the reverse idler shaft. It holds the reverse gear, which, when engaged, between the countershaft and the output shaft makes the output shaft rotate in the opposite direction to the input shaft.

Just to put aside a common misconception, with the exception of the reverse idler gear, the gears are in constant mesh with each other, they do not move to engage with each other. Each gearwheel adjacent to a synchro hub is carried on needle bearings.

Gear combinations are changed via forks, each permanently engaged with a single synchro hub, controlled by the car's gear (shift) lever. In order to achieve smoother and quicker gear changes, synchronisers are used. Each synchroniser consists of a hub (engaged by splines with the shaft carrying it and again by splines to the outer coupling sleeve) and two baulk rings (or clutches), one on each side. The outer coupling sleeve is able to move laterally under the influence of the selector fork engaged in the groove that runs around its circumference.

The synchroniser's main function is to synchronize (equalize) the rotation speed of the gearwheel it wants to select with the speed of the shaft carrying that gear. This is achieved when the tapered shoulder of the baulk ring presses against a matching tapered shoulder on the side of the gear. When rotational speeds are matched, the synchroniser's coupling sleeve is able to fully engage the gear and lock it to the shaft in order to transmit drive.

A modern five-speed gearbox

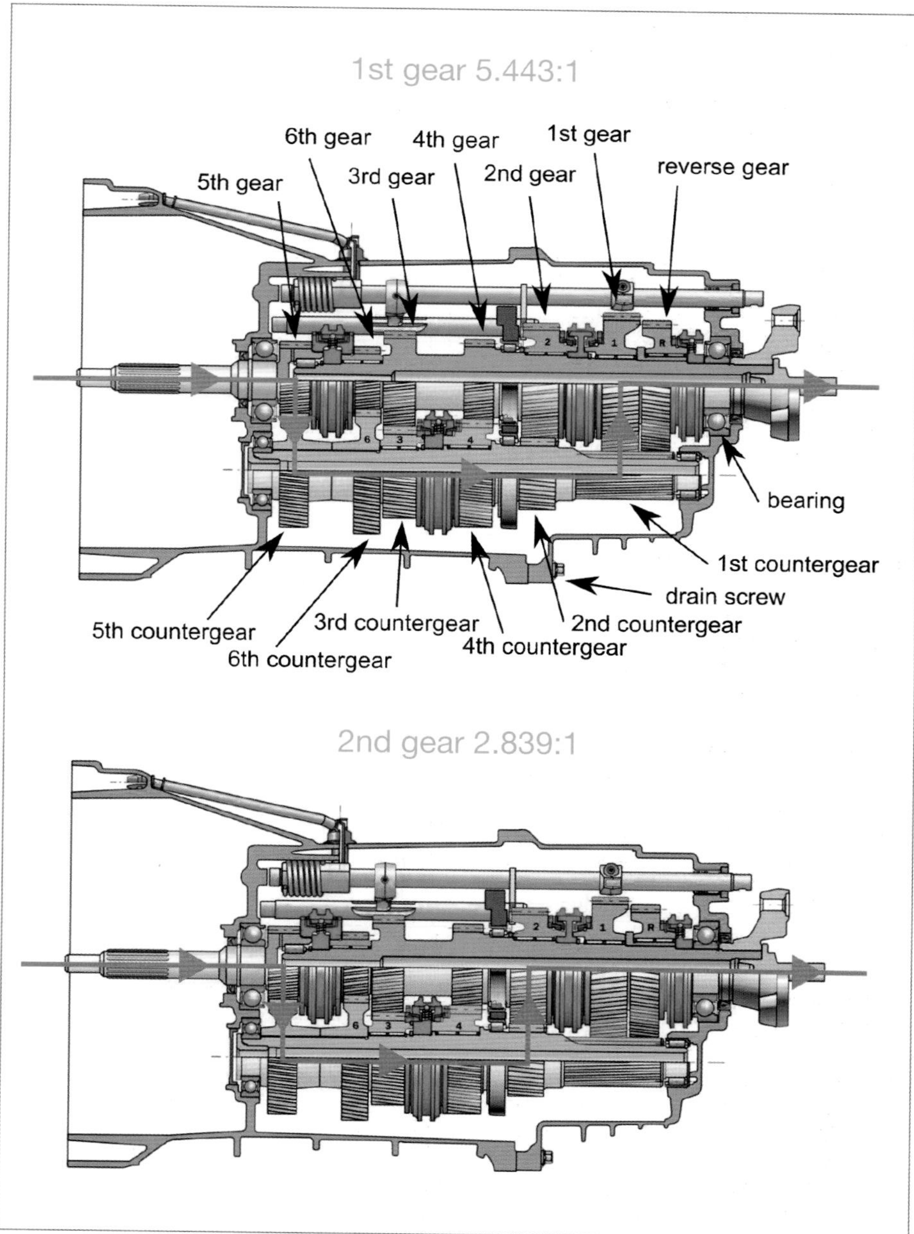

Fig 55 (pages 59-62): How the power flows through a six-speed manual gearbox/transmission unit depending on which gear is selected. (Courtesy Land Rover)

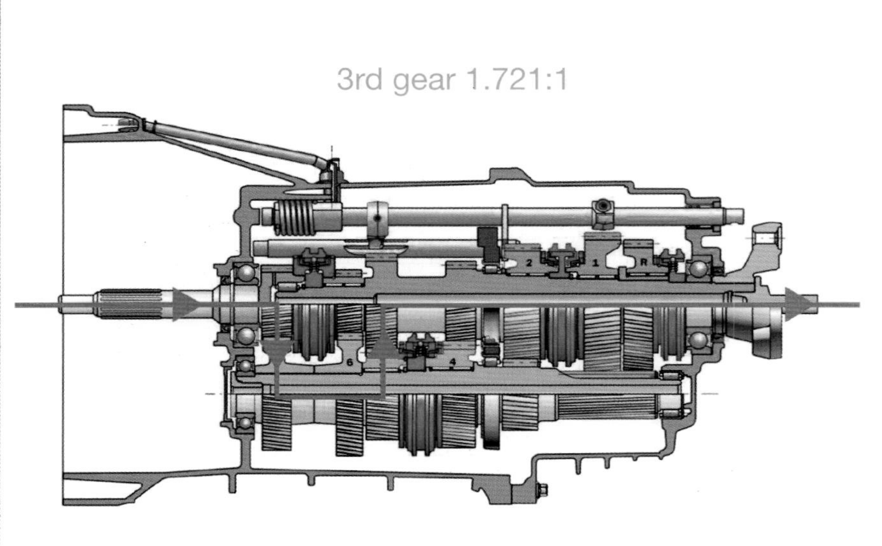
3rd gear 1.721:1
2
1
R
6
4

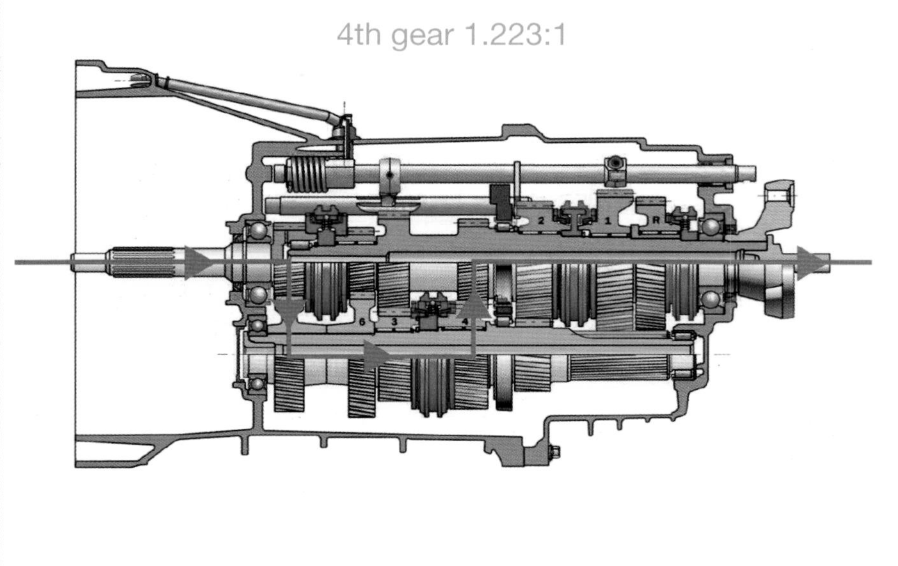
4th gear 1.223:1
2
1
R
6
3
4

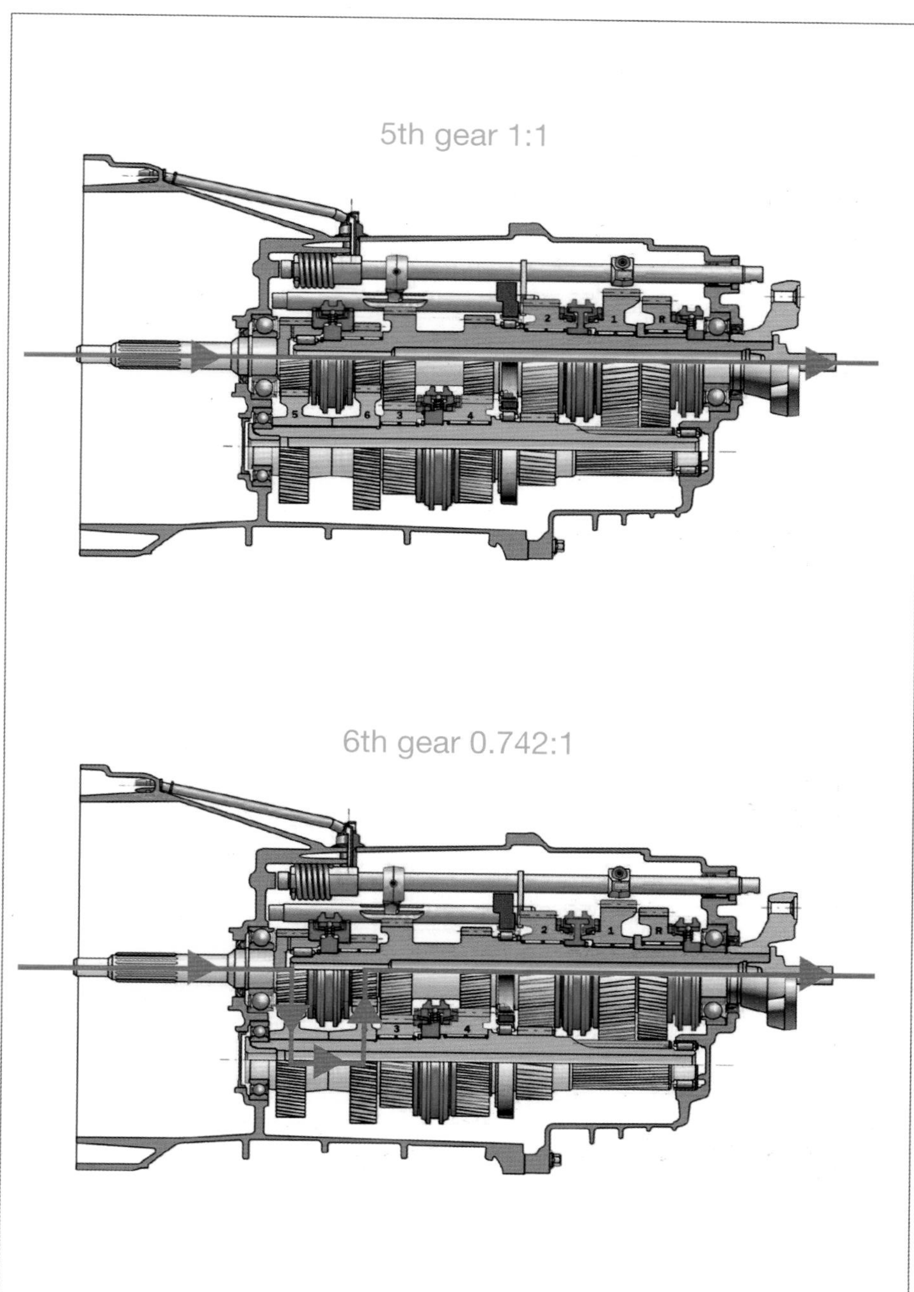
5th gear 1:1
2
1
R
5
6
3
4
6th gear 0.742:1
2
1
R
3
4

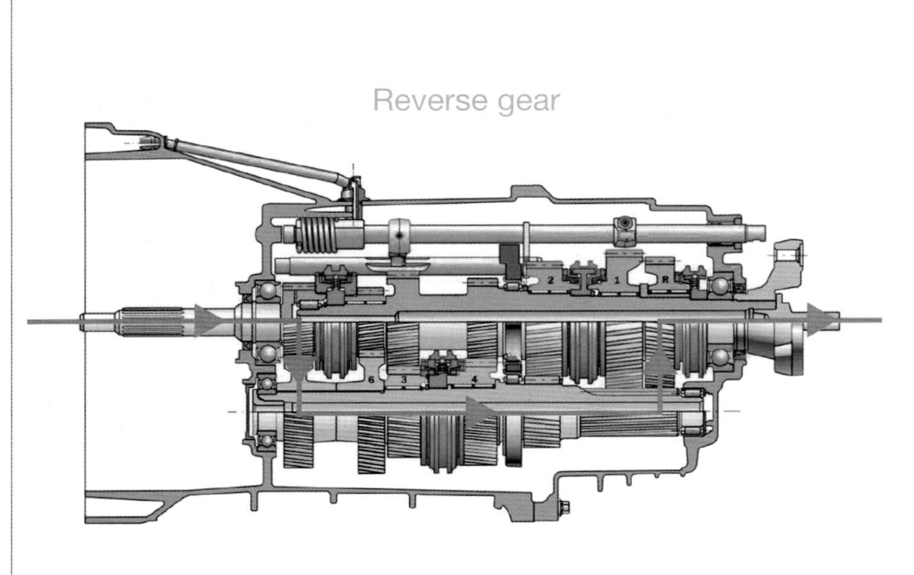
Reverse gear

Neutral

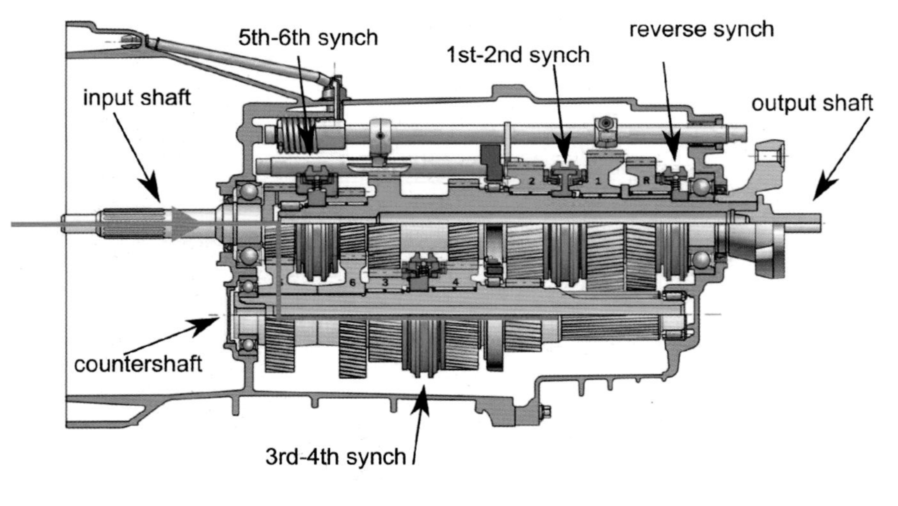
5th-6th synch
reverse synch
1st-2nd synch
input shaft
output shaft
countershaft
3rd-4th synch

with reverse below fifth will have three synchronizers: first to second gear, third to fourth, and fifth/reverse synchroniser.

The gears work immersed in transmission oil, which provides lubrication and cooling by transferring the heat from the gears to the gearbox casing

Automatic transmission

Fig 56 & 57. Cars with automatic transmission do not require a clutch, instead a 'torque converter' provides a coupling/de-coupling mechanism between the engine and transmission. Gears are changed automatically, the driver simply selecting the mode which is usually one of three: 'D' – drive, 'P' – park or 'R' – reverse.

The torque converter is, in effect, a fluid clutch, where the driving fan, connected to the engine, drives automatic transmission fluid (ATF) to the driven fan, connected to the gearbox, forcing it to revolve. When the engine is idling and the driving fan turns only slowly, it direct fluid with enough force to make the driven fan turn. As engine revs rise, the driven fan begins to rotate, but is initially slower than the driving fan because of slip. Once underway, the driven fan's speed will be virtually the same as the driving fan's, but not quite 1:1 and that why automatic transmission cars are less economical than manual gearbox cars. The gradual convergence in speed between the two fans is the torque conversion and it allows power to be smoothly transmitted to the gearbox. A stator

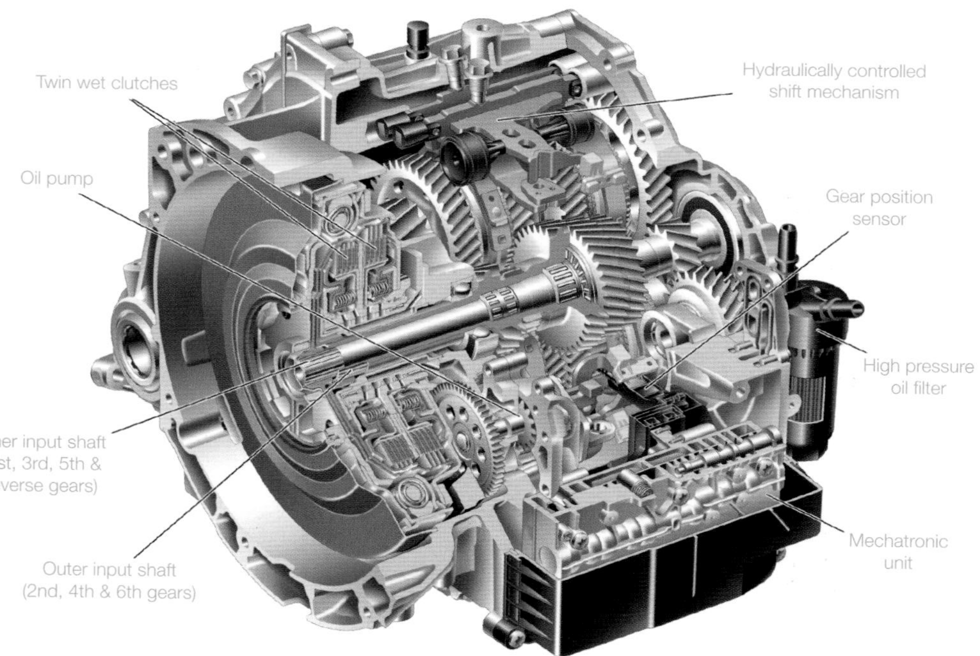

Fig 56: A cross-section view of a modern automatic gearbox. (Courtesy Volvo)

	Automatic transmission gear selection sequence			
	Sun gear	**Planetary gears**	**Ring gear**	**What happens?**
1	Input	Held	Held	Direct, gear ratio 1:1
2	Driven	Held	Input	Overdrive in reverse
3	Input	Held	Driven	Reduced gear in reverse
4	Held	Input	Driven	Overdrive
5	Held	Driven	Input	Gear reduction
6	Input	Driven	Held	Gear reduction
7	Driven	Input	Held	Overdrive
8	Input	Driven	Driven	Neutral

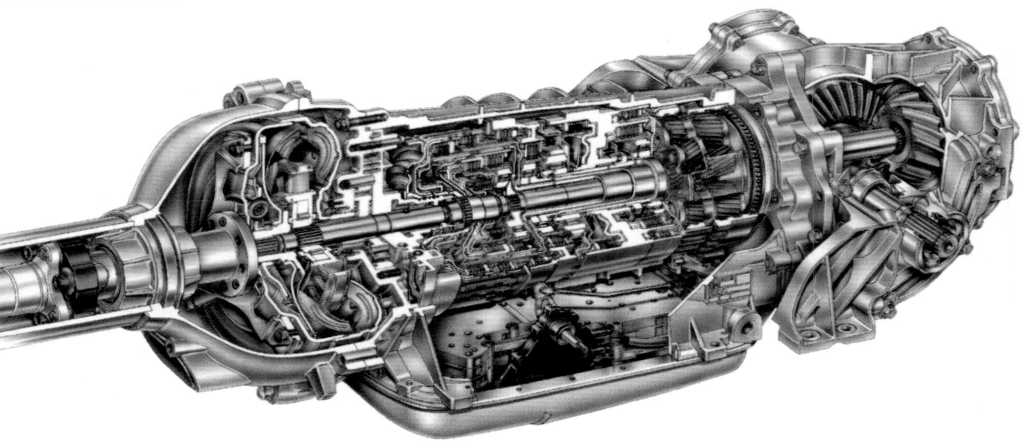

Fig 57: An interestingly constructed automatic transmission unit. Unlike most, this one is located at the back of the vehicle just in front of the rear axle. You can see the differential unit mounted directly onto the back of the transmission casing. This Cadillac transmission unit is said to be very quiet and vibration-free. (Courtesy David Kimble via Cadillac Media Division)

between the two fans helps improve the fluid flow and prevent power loss.

Gear changes in an automatic transmission are carried out by a planetary gearset. This consists of a large ring gear, planet gears rotating inside the ring gear, and a sun gear in the centre of the system. Additionally, there is the planet carrier that holds the 'planets' in place, and translates their movement to a shaft. Although at first glance there appears to be only one way to move a planetary gearset, there are actually eight possible combinations, depending on which element you hold and which one you couple with the engine input. Truly magical! In practice, only six of these combinations are used. Thus we forget about combinations two and four.

To make it possible to hold certain elements of the planetary gearset and switch between input and output, small clutches powered by a sophisticated hydraulic valve mechanism are needed. The valve mechanism, usually located underneath the gearbox, receives information from the oil pump, which is located between the gearbox and the torque convertor. According to what is happening in the torque converter, the oil pump outputs the appropriate pressure. This is how information about engine speed is transmitted to the valve mechanism. The valves 'read' the oil pump's pressure, and engage or disengage the clutches to switch between the various combinations of the planetary gearset. Although it is possible to make a gearbox with just one planetary gearset, the modern multispeed boxes will have two or even three to improve efficiency, give a wider variation of gear ratios, and decrease the shifting intervals.

An automatic transmission unit tends to overheat quickly. Although it is fluid that drives the torque converter, there is still friction between particles, and any friction, of course, produces heat. Some cars have a dedicated cooling system to deal with the transmission only, however, the majority of road vehicles will have a system that pumps the heated transmission oil to a lower (and separate) part of the engine's radiator, where it is cooled before being returned to the transmission. A new vehicle with new generation ATF, theoretically, should be good to drive for 100,000 miles without a change, but it is strongly recommended that the manufacturer's maintenance schedule is followed.

Automatic transmission, although capable of dealing various driving situations on its own, can still take commands from the driver. That's why there are several driving modes on the gear lever: 'D' (Drive) is the normal driving mode for auto transmission cars. When the gear (shift) lever is in this mode, the transmission will use its own judgement about shifting gears. It will go from first upwards as the car's speed increases. 'S' (Sport) – if available, this mode will hold each gear a little longer (to higher engine revs) to achieve faster acceleration. 'P' (Park) – this locks the transmission, however, it doesn't mean that you can ignore the parking brake. 'N' (Neutral) – no gear is selected and no power is transmitted to the wheels. In order to start an auto transmission car, you need to put the lever in 'N' or 'P.' Unfortunately, the driver still has to make the effort of selecting reverse. Sometimes there are additional numbered modes, like '1' '2' or '3' – these allow the driver to limit the transmission's gear changing. For example, if you approach a steep hill or drive in adverse weather conditions, it can makes sense to select '2' so that the gearbox won't shift any higher than second gear, providing high torque to the driven wheels.

Semi-automatic transmission

A semi-automatic transmission is found on some high performance vehicles like Porsches and Ferraris. Technically, it is still a proper manual transmission, with the only difference being that the driver doesn't have to use a clutch to change gear. The clutch is still in place, but there's no clutch pedal. There is a gear (shift) lever or, sometimes, buttons or paddles on the steering wheel. All mechanical movements previously performed by the driver are now performed by an electronic 'brain' and its pneumatic 'arms.' Various sensors gather information about engine speed and driver gear choice, triggering the operation of a sophisticated system that disengages the clutch, shifts the gears, then re-engages the clutch; all whilst simultaneously matching the engine revs to achieve a smoother shift.

Drive types

The drive is the mechanism that transfers the power from the output of the transmission to the driven wheels. There are various drive types.

Rear-wheel drive

Fig 58. The classic layout incorporates an engine at the front of the car driving the rear wheels. It's a very easy and straightforward system. Easy to manufacture, and easy to maintain.

The driveshaft (or propshaft), a long sturdy steel shaft, connects the gearbox (transmission) ouput to the rear axle assembly through two, or more, flexible joints. The joint at the rear of the transmission is called a slip joint. The part that turns the driveshaft can slide backwards and forwards on the transmission output shaft, as matching splines enable slight horizontal movement. If there was no slip joint, the rear suspension movements would cause the driveshaft to push or pull on the gearbox output shaft.

At both ends of the driveshaft there's a universal joint which permits movement in both horizontal and vertical planes, again to allow for the movement created by the rear suspension.

Fig 59. Power is transferred to the rear wheels through the rear axle assembly, consisting of a crownwheel and pinion, differential unit, and halfshafts. Drive from the engine enters the differential case via the driveshaft from the gearbox. The input shaft has a pinion gear engaged with a large ring gear (the 'crownwheel') on one side, and, by this means, the drive changes direction by 90 degrees. A differential cage is mounted in the ring gear and rotates with it. Two satellite pinion gears are located inside the differential cage. Both halfshafts (they power the wheels) end inside the differential cage, and are connected to each other via the satellite gears. As the differential cage rotates, so do the halfshafts. When one shaft is locked, the other one will still be able to rotate – the satellite gears will orbit

Fig 58: A classic drivetrain – engine at the front, rear wheels driven via the gearbox (1), driveshaft (propshaft) (2), differential (3), and rear axle drive shafts (halfshafts) (4). This rear axle has independent suspension. (Courtesy General Motors)

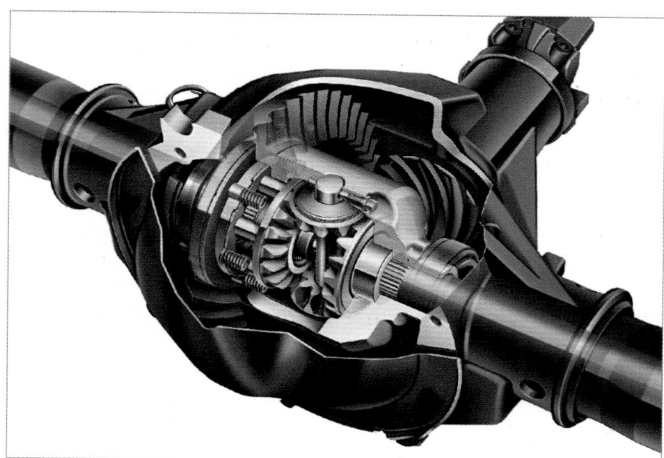

Fig 59: Inside the differential case of a solid rear axle with internal halfshafts carrying power to the rear wheels. Holding one wheel to slow its rotation will cause the two satellite gears to rotate around the drive gear of the slowed halfshaft, in the process increasing the speed of the drive to the halfshaft powering the other wheel. (Courtesy General Motors)

around the locked shaft's pinion gear. This clever system also permits both halfshafts to turn at different speeds. This differential effect is needed when making turns, as the outside wheels will need to travel further and, therefore, turn faster than the inside wheel.

When the differential case is fixed directly to the car's chassis/body, swing axles are used to allow for suspension movements. Swing axles connect the differential to the wheels. They have universal joints of various designs at both wheel hub and differential case ends, permitting movement in both horizontal and vertical planes.

Four-wheel drive (4WD)

On a 4WD car the rear drive looks pretty much like the classic system already described. However, an additional driveshaft will supply power from the gearbox (transmission) to a second axle (front or rear, depending on engine/gearbox location and engine orientation). The second powered axle will also require a differential.

Four wheel drive systems come with various levels of sophistication, some are permanent, meaning that all four wheels are driven at all times. Some allow one axle to be disengaged (for economy's sake) at the pull of a lever, touch of a button, or even manually by twisting a key at the front wheel hubs. Others are able to vary torque between front and rear axles and even at individual wheels, automatically adapting to prevailing conditions.

Fig 60. 4WD cars intended for serious off-road use are equipped with a differential lock. This is a mechanism that stops the wheels on a single axle turning at different speeds and also

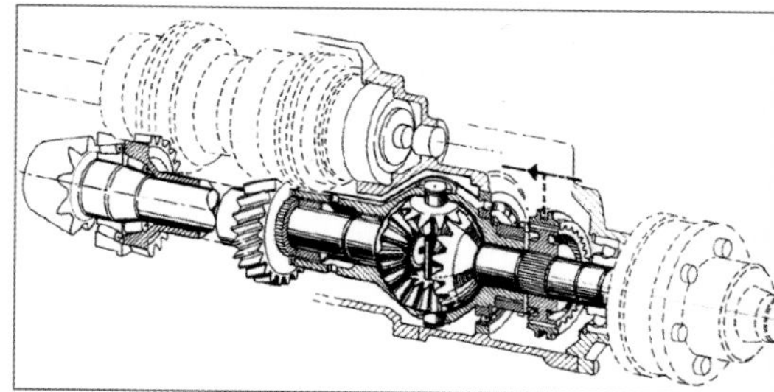

Fig 60: Differential lock. Note the arrow. Once the lock slides to the left, both axles are locked together. Now they cannot have variable speeds, and are forced to turn together. (Courtesy Audi)

Fig 61. Four-wheel drive. Note the transfer drive from the gearbox (1) to the differential unit (2), and the driveshafts (3) powering the front wheels. (Courtesy General Motors)

will not allow one wheel to stop turning whist the other spins. On a normal differential, thanks to the satellite gears, each wheel can turn at its own speed (remember, we need this feature when the car is cornering). When you get into a mud pit or deep snow and one of the wheels loses traction, it will start spinning much faster without actually doing any useful work. By engaging a differential lock, both wheels are forced to turn at equal speeds. In most cases traction will be regained and help you out of the mud pit. However, the differential lock must be engaged only when really necessary. Some cars use automatic differential locks, which will engage each time the system detects one wheel losing traction.

Some people mistakenly use the term 'locking differential' when actually referring to a 'limited-slip' differential. Locking differentials and limited-slip differentials are not the same thing. Limited-slip differentials use a series of clutch plates to disengage the differential's satellite gears when one of the wheels loses traction. It is not as efficient as a differential lock, but does allow the vehicle to be steered and driven normally. It's a popular system for rally cars.

Fig 62: Front-wheel drive, but not a transverse engine layout. 1 Flywheel, 2 Clutch, 3 Input shaft, 4 Countershaft, 5 Output shaft, 6 Differential, 7 & 8 Power to the front wheels. (Courtesy Audi)

Front-wheel drive

A front wheel drive system offers some advantages over the classic rear-wheel drive system. For example, there's no need for a driveshaft (propshaft) running to the rear of the vehicle (or a transmission tunnel within the passenger compartment). Front-wheel drive cars can have better traction (grip on the road) because the drive wheels have more weight upon them (the engine and transaxle).

To allow front-wheel drive, the engine is best installed transversely (east west) so that there is no need to turn the drive through 90 degrees before it reaches the wheels. Nevertheless, there are some cars that have the engine placed longitudinally (north south).

Fig 62. The engine on a front-wheel drive car is coupled with a transaxle unit (a combination of gearbox and differential).

The output shaft of the gearbox drives the ring gear of the differential unit, then power flows to the axle shafts to drive the front wheels. The drive shafts that transfer power to the front wheels have universal joints at both ends to make steering possible and to allow suspension movement.

Wheels and tyres (tires)

Wheels

The wheel is a simple yet truly magical device, capable of translating rotational movement into linear movement. It also supports the weight of the car.

A modern wheel is a metal cylinder whose outer rim has a certain profile for additional strength and to hold the tyre in place.

Traditional steel wheels are made of two pressings welded together. They can look quite plain, which is why wheel covers are often used. Many modern cars have aluminium alloy wheels which come in a huge variety of styles and sizes. Alloy wheels also tend to be lighter than steel ones.

The wheel will incorporate a valve to allow inflation of the tyre.

Fig 63. The wheels are mounted on a hub: a cylindrical component with a disc-shaped flange. The hub's task is to provide a fixing plate for the wheel. The hubs of non-driving wheels revolve freely around a stationary stub axle (a spindle) on a pair of ball bearings or roller bearings. The stub axle is usually fixed to an 'upright' between two horizontal arms ('wishbones'), or to a suspension strut. Sideways movement of the hub is restricted by a heavy washer and a lock nut that sits on the outer end of the stub axle. For driven wheels, the driveshaft passes through bearings within a combination hub/upright, usually carried between two horizontal suspension arms or, sometimes, a suspension strut. There will be a universal joint inboard of the hub. On a 4WD or front-wheel drive car, the setup is usually as just described except that, for the front wheels, the hub through which the driveshaft passes is able to swivel laterally to allow for steering movements.

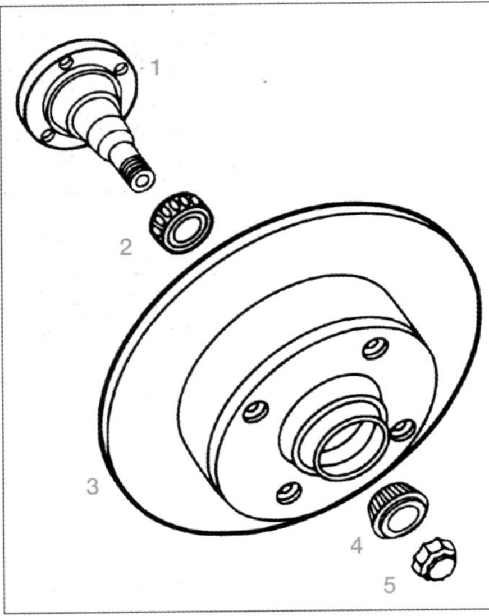

Fig 63: A simplified wheel hub scheme. 1 Spindle/stub axle, 2 Inner taper bearing, 3 Wheel hub with the brake disc, 4 Outer taper bearing, 5 Lock nut.

Tyres (tires)

The tyre (tire) is mounted directly on the wheel. Rubber tyres add to the comfort of the passengers and, in conjunction with the suspension, cushion the car from road bumps. However, the main function of the tyre is to provide traction with the road surface. Rubber and tarmac work well together.

Fig 64. Modern tyres do not require inner tubes as wall of a tubeless tyre forms a non-leaking bond with the wheel rim through a tyre bead within which is a strong woven metal wire hoop. The bond is also helped by the fact that rubber is rather elastic. Once inflated, the tubeless tyre is held in place by the internal air pressure and the safety ridges on the wheel rim's profile.

Fig 65. Tubeless tyres, unless they suffer a big gash, are largely protected from small punctures by a self-sealing layer located inside the tyre.

Fig 64: This is how a tubeless tyre is mounted on an aluminium wheel. In this instance the rubber band around the centre of the rim ensures you can still limp to the service station even after a severe puncture. Very few cars have this feature. (Courtesy Audi)

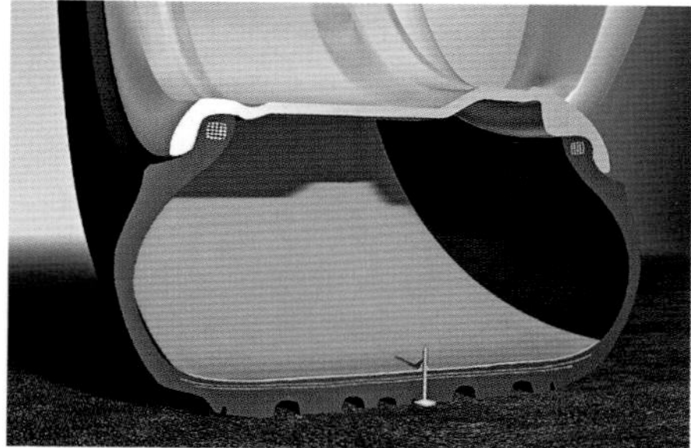

Fig 65: The self-healing layer in a Continental tyre. (Courtesy Continental

Fig 66: A good tyre will dispose of water through side exit treads, and so prevent aquaplaning. (Courtesy Uniroyal Tyres)

Fig 66. The patterned surface of the tyre which come into contact with the road is called the tread. The tread pattern is there to increase the grip by expelling water quickly in wet weather to reduce the possibility of aquaplaning (when the tread sits on a cushion of water and loses direct contact with the road).

Fig 67: Multiple layers at various cord directions on a large modern 4x4 vehicle tyre. (Courtesy Bridgestone)

Fig 67. Beneath the treaded surface of the tyre there are several layers, or plies, to strengthen the casing in various directions. Each layer contains threads or cords. Tyres are classified by the direction of the cords. Most modern road cars are equipped with 'radial' tyres. The cords in the plies run in a radial direction, that is across the crown of the tyre at right angles to the direction of wheel travel and from one bead to the other, the tyre's carcass will also incorporate radial cords. For extra stability, breaker belts with diagonal cords can also be incorporated.

On the sidewall of a tyre numbers and messages give a great deal of information. The tyre size usually looks like this example: 'P195/80 R14.'

'P' indicates that it is for a passenger vehicle.

'195' is the height of the sidewall in millimetres.

'80' is the aspect ratio between height and width of the tyre (low-profile tyres will have a lower aspect ratio).

'R' stands for 'radial.'

'14' indicates the wheel diameter in inches.

Properly inflated tyres will reduce rolling resistance (saving fuel), optimise road holding, reduce braking distances and prolong tyre life. The car manufacturer's recommendations regarding front and rear tyre pressures should always be followed.

Wheel alignment

Although at first glance it may seem that all four wheels are perfectly parallel with each other and perfectly vertical, there are actually slight angles everywhere, and there's a good reason for this.

Caster

Fig 68. If you were to draw a line through the two points about which a front wheel pivots, and extend it to the road surface, you would see that, in most cases, it hits a point in the road ahead of the tyre's contact patch. This geometry creates a trailing effect (like the wheels of a supermarket trolley) as it makes the wheel prefer to run straight in the direction of travel.

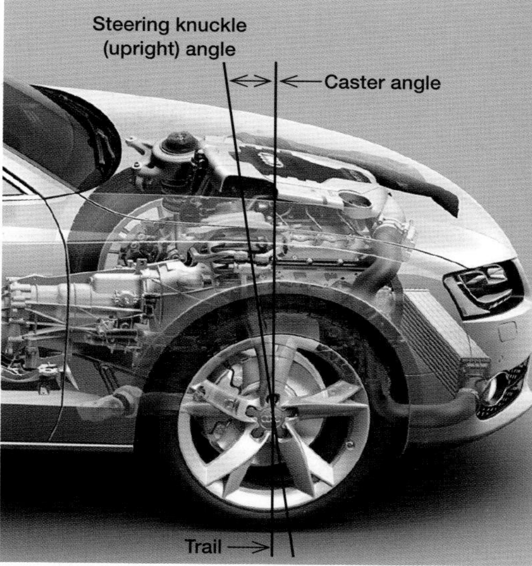

Fig 68. An illustration of positive caster and how it creates trail. (Background image Courtesy Audi).

Camber

Fig 69. When observed from the front or rear of the car, camber refers to the inward or outward vertical tilt of the wheels.

The camber angle is required to compensate for the weight of the car's load; also for body roll and changes to suspension geometry during cornering. Camber may be positive (wheels lean inward from bottom to top), or negative (wheels lean outward from bottom to top), depending on the design of the car's suspension system.

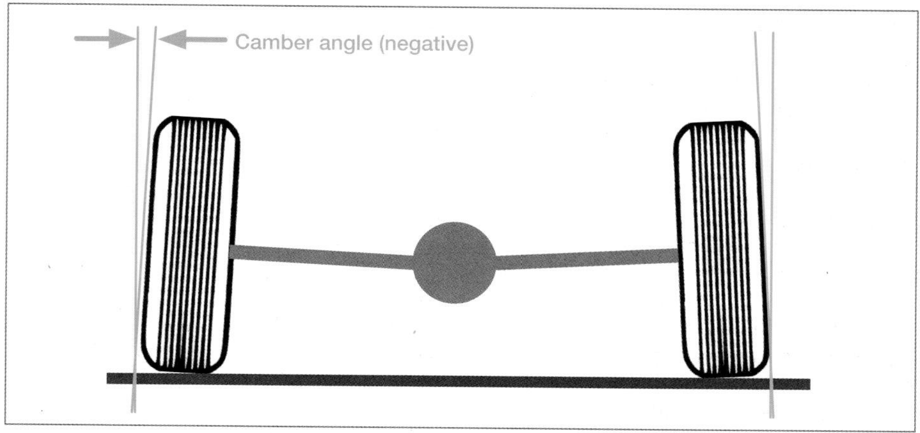

Fig 69: Negative camber shown here. If the wheels were leaning outward at the top, they would have positive camber.

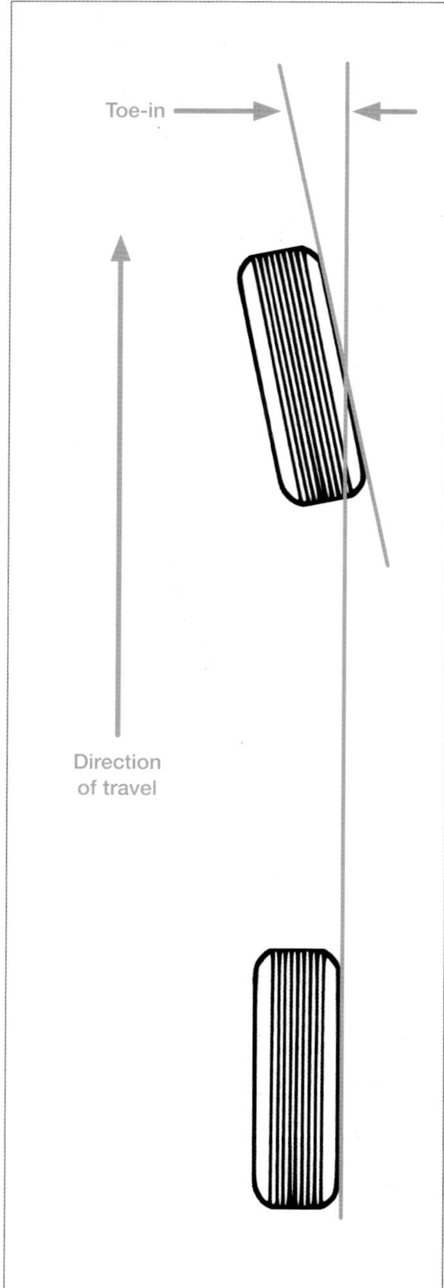

Fig 70: Toe-in shown here on the right-hand side of a car. If the front wheel was angled outward, rather than inward, it would have toe out.

Toe

Fig 70. Toe is the inward or outward horizontal angle of the wheels. Front-wheel drive and rear-wheel drive cars require different toe settings. On a rear-wheel drive car, natural forces (rolling resistance/braking) push the fronts of the wheels apart, or to 'toe-out.' In order to compensate for this effect, they are set to 'toe-in,' when static to compensate for the natural forces applied in use.

On a front-wheel drive car, the fronts of the front wheels will be forced together (a toe-in tendency). That's why we need to adjust these front wheels to toe-out when static. The amount of toe adjustment is usually just a very small number of degrees.

Ackermann angle

Fig 71. This is closely related to the toe. When a car is turning, the turning radius of the inner wheel is smaller than that of the outer wheel. This needs to be compensated for to improve cornering and reduce tyre wear.

Ackermann's angle geometry is built into the steering system so that it is automatically applied when cornering. So, for every degree you turn the front outer wheel, the front inner one will turn a little bit more.

Tracking

Tracking is not really an angle, rather it is a measure of the mutual alignment of all four-wheels. Normal tracking adjustment ensures that the rear wheels will follow the tracks of the front wheels. Adjusting tracking is quite tricky and is best left to professionals.

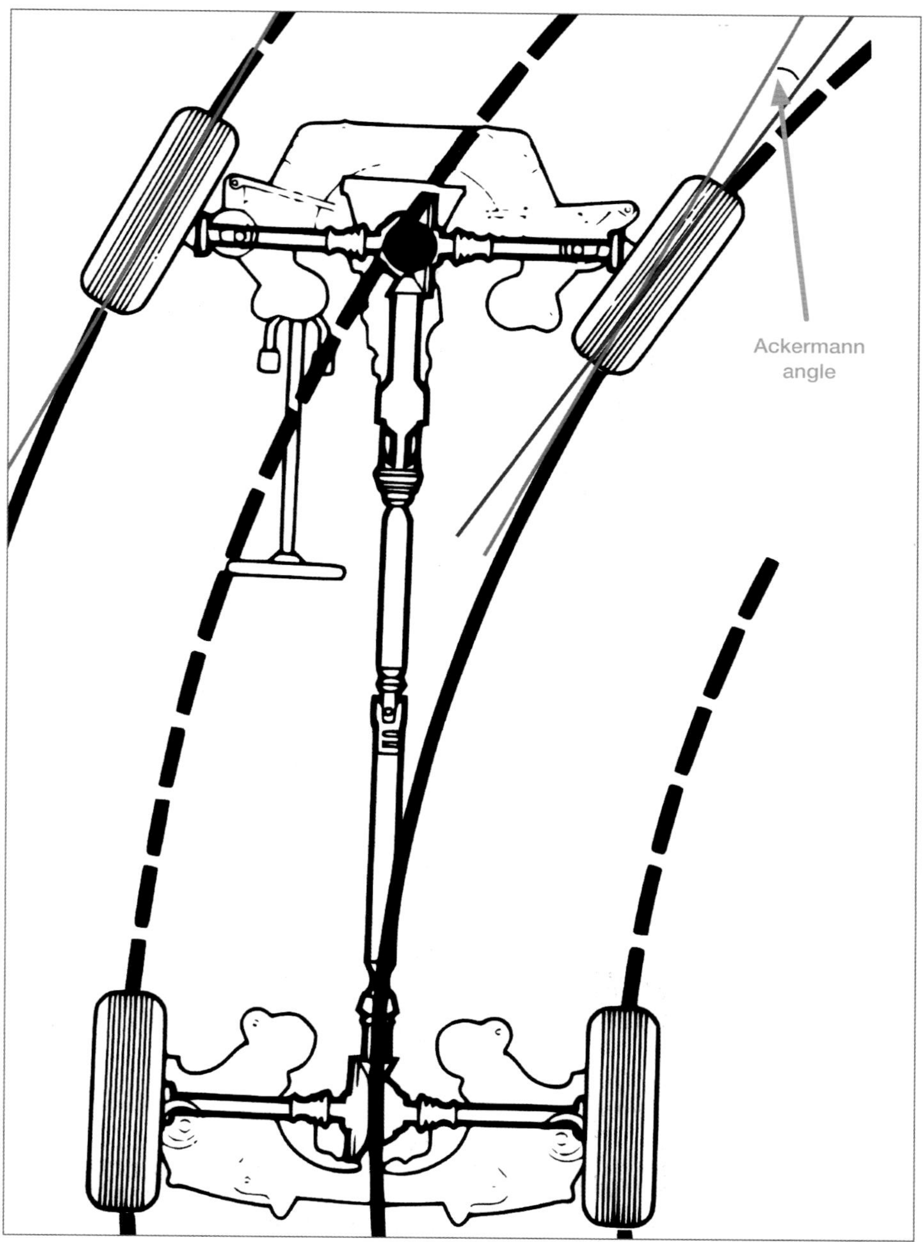

Fig 71: The Ackermann angle built into the steering system's geometry ensures the inner wheel follows a smaller radius during a turn.

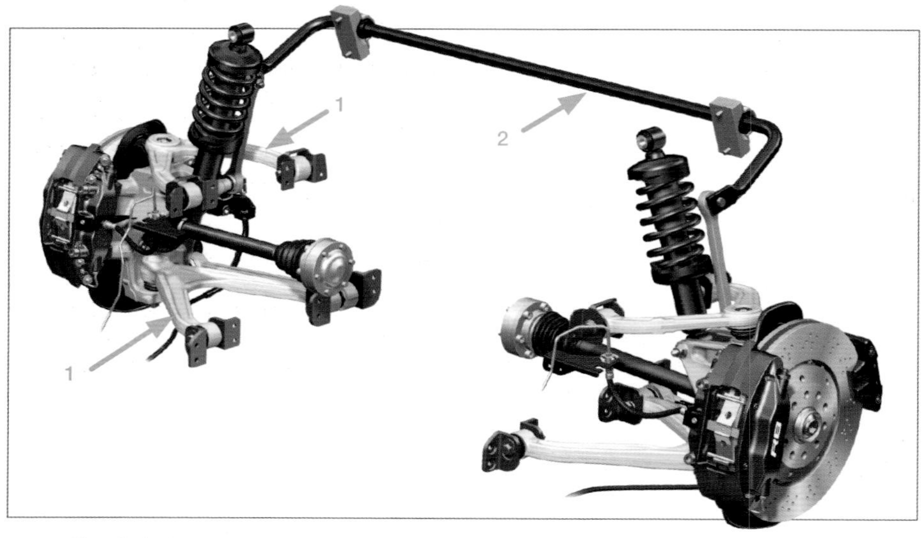

Fig 72: A double wishbone (1) suspension unit with an anti-roll bar (2). (Courtesy Audi)

Fig 73: MacPherson strut (1)-type suspension. Also take a look at the interesting construction of the collapsible steering column (2) in the background. (Courtesy General Motors)

Suspension system

The main function of the suspension is to support the car body weight, provide a smooth ride, and keep the wheels firmly pressed against the road. It also prevents the car from swaying and tilting excessively during cornering, braking and acceleration.

A basic suspension system consists

of a spring, a shock absorber (actually a damper), and a system of control arms that connect the wheels and their associated components to the vehicle frame. The control arms have the ability to swing up and down following the movement of the wheel. The inboard parts of the suspension are attached to the car's chassis frame, or to the monocoque underbody.

A suspension spring can take many forms and shapes. The one that makes the most sense is a coil spring. Due to its shape, it can be mounted directly over the shock absorber, thus saving space. Leaf springs are still occasionally used to provide rear suspension.

The shock absorbers (also more accurately called dampers) are constructed similarly to an office chair's central leg. Essentially, these are telescopic devices designed to resist vertical movement in both directions; in other words to dampen the natural oscillation of the springs that would occur without the resistance provided by the shock absorber. Modern shock absorbers are gas-filled pneumatic devices, whilst older designs are oil-filled hydraulic devices.

Front suspension

The steering swivel member (upright) connects to the suspension control arms (usually 'wishbones') via two ball joints (one ball joint if the suspension is in strut form), making both steering and vertical movement possible.

Double wishbone suspension

Fig 72. Double-wishbone suspension is popular, and is a system whereby the wheel is 'suspended' on an upright between the tips of two parallel, and usually wishbone-shaped, control arms attached to the car's frame. The lower wishbone usually supports the swivel member (or 'upright'), the spring and shock absorber, while the upper wishbone supports just the steering swivel member. The 'parallel' nature of the two wishbones ensures the wheel maintains a vertical position as the suspension moves up and down. In fact, although the wishbones may look parallel, there is actually a slight angle between them, and the upper wishbone is a little shorter than the lower one. This geometry is needed so that the wheel top can tilt inward when the tyre goes over a bump.

MacPherson strut suspension

Fig 73. An alternative suspension system is the MacPherson strut, or derivatives of it. It uses a substantially longer shock absorber body (the strut), and the spring is incorporated on the exterior of the strut. The upper end of the strut assembly is attached to the car's body in a relatively high position. If you look at the bodywork inside the car's engine compartment, you'll see two large bulges on each side – that's where the struts are mounted to the body.

In a MacPherson strut suspension system the lower wishbone (or its equivalent) is still there, but the upper wishbone has been replaced by the strut which is also the swivel member.

The MacPherson system is much simpler, and offers an obvious advantage – three functions in one unit and the wheel camber (inward/outward tilt) stays within reasonable limits, adding to passenger comfort.

Anti-roll bar

Fig 72. Another aid to passenger comfort is an anti-roll bar or torsion bar. It is connected to both sides of the car's frame, and to both sides of the front suspension (usually the lower parts of the struts on a MacPherson set up

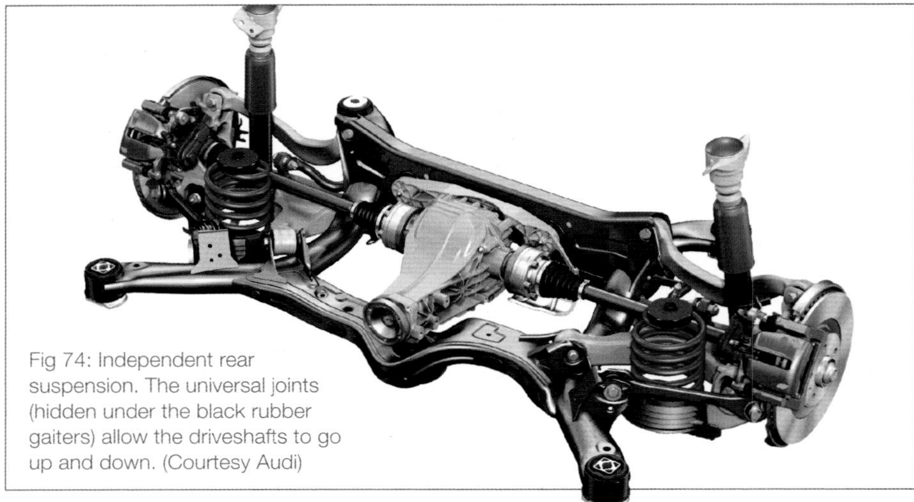

Fig 74: Independent rear suspension. The universal joints (hidden under the black rubber gaiters) allow the driveshafts to go up and down. (Courtesy Audi)

and the lower wishbone of a double wishbone setup).

The anti-roll bar resists the rolling that occurs during cornering when weight is transferred to the outer springs. The bar will twist, but will resist the twist and keep the car's body as level as possible.

High-end cars, however, can feature an electronic suspension control unit that not only controls the degree of damping effect from the shock absorbers, but also regulates the amount of body roll. For example, if you restrict body roll on a 4WD car too much, it will lose some of its off-road ability because its suspension won't be able to move as freely as it needs to. To overcome this problem an expensive 4WD car will have the anti-roll bar designed as a series of arms whose position is regulated by a control unit. This system will resist rolling in urban environments, but allow more freedom in off-road mode.

Rear suspension

Fig 74. Most of the cars produced during the last couple of decades will have an independent rear suspension system, where each wheel is given a certain amount of freedom so that it can move up and down without affecting the other rear wheel. Non-independent suspension has a solid axle connecting both rear wheels – one wheel reacting to a bump inevitably affects its companion on the same axle.

When cars are equipped with a rigid rear axle, it is usually attached to the car's body via leaf springs and shock absorbers. Thanks to the universal joints at each end of the driveshaft (propshaft), the rigid axle can move up and down. However, a better level of comfort is achieved by using independent rear suspension.

Unlike rigid rear axles, the differential casing of an independent suspension system is fixed to the frame or underbody of the car. Each of the driveshafts connecting the differential unit to the rear wheels has two universal joints, allowing the suspension to move while the differential casing stays still.

Each rear wheel will be supported by two swinging arms (wishbones), similar to the ones already described for the front suspension. The wishbones are mounted at their wide end to the car's frame on sturdy pivots, whilst their tips are attached to a wheel hub upright which cannot swivel. Thus, only up and down movement is possible.

Coil springs and shock absorbers are usually attached to the lower wishbones and the car's frame. It's also possible to use a MacPherson strut-type suspension at the rear, where the coil spring is in unit with the shock absorber and only a single wishbone or equivalent is required.

De Dion system

The De Dion system has the differential casing attached to the body and the driveshafts, which are set free to move up and down by universal joints. So far, it sounds like an independent suspension system, but it's not because there are no wishbones. The rear wheels hubs are instead firmly connected by a large metal tube which holds the rear wheels in parallel. De Dion suspension is cheaper than independent suspension, and offers a better ride than non-independant suspension. It is still used by smaller car manufacturers and kit car makers, and is also seen on some larger 4WD vehicles.

Steering system

Every car will have a steering wheel that turns the front wheels by converting its rotational movement into linear movement.

Because the front wheels have to bear so much weight, it can be difficult to steer them with muscle power alone. That's where power steering comes in handy.

A basic steering mechanism consists of a steering wheel, steering

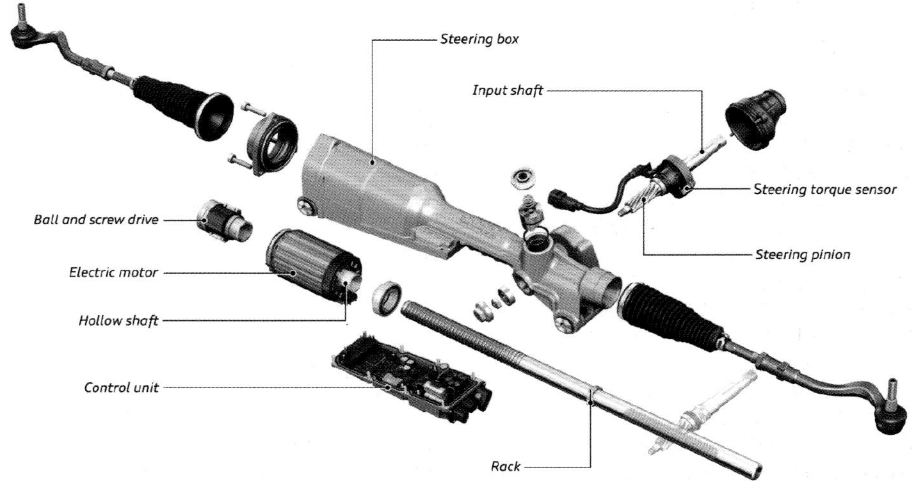

Fig 75: A rack and pinion power steering system with the power assist coming from an electric motor. As the system senses the driver turning the steering wheel, the electric motor starts to turn in the necessary direction, screwing the rack to left or right. The electric motor's rotor drives the ball and screw drive, which applies force to the rack. (Courtesy Audi)

shaft, and a steering rack or a steering box and arm mechanism. There are usually two or more universal joints in the steering column, joining several shafts together. Not only do these joints allow the column to find its way around various awkwardly placed components in the engine bay, it can also facilitate steering wheel adjustment (if available), whereby you can move the steering wheel into the position that best suits your size and driving style.

Steering box

This is a frame-mounted steering gearbox at the end of the steering column, designed to make the steering lighter. The idea is that a larger gear turns a smaller gear, thus increasing torque and making it easier to steer, although slowing steering response.

In many designs the steering wheel turns a worm gear, which transfers the movement to a pinion gear attached to the output arm (also called the drop arm). The drop arm governs two interconnected arms that relay the intended direction of turn to the steering swivels. A steering gearbox has a very high gear ratio, typically 15:1 to 20:1.

Rack and pinion

Fig 75. With a rack and pinion steering system, the rotational movement of the steering wheel is transferred to the frame-mounted rack and pinion steering assembly. The pinion turns in response to the driver's input and shifts the rack to the left or right. In turn, the rack moves the track rod arms that are connected to the steering swivel member. The simple rack and pinion mechanism gives very precise steering, but a considerable amount of muscle power is needed to move the wheels.

Power steering

Fig 75. The majority of modern cars are equipped with power steering. Today's power steering mechanisms are usually powered by an engine-driven pump and a hydraulic servo system.

Based on a rack and pinion unit, the rack housing is a sealed system kept under constant high pressure by the pump. The rack has a piston attached near one end, to both sides of which hydraulic pressure can be applied. The steering shaft enters the rack housing via a valve body that controls the bias of hydraulic pressure. As you turn the steering wheel, you open the particular power steering valve (the left or right one), and the pressure is applied to one face of the piston. If pressure is applied on the left side of the piston, the car will turn right, and vice versa. As a backup system, the good old rack and pinion is still in place so, if the power steering packs up, you're still able to limp back to the service station on muscle power alone.

Electric and electro-hydraulic systems are making an appearance. They, like traditional systems, apply additional turning power to assist the driver in response to steering input.

Braking system

Although drum and disc brakes have been around for a long time, we still don't have anything better.

Even though drum brakes are less efficient, they are still sometimes used on all four wheels. However, it is more common to find disc brakes at the front of the car and drum brakes at the rear.

There's really nothing wrong with drum brakes at the rear because it's the front brakes that have to be more powerful. During braking a dynamic weight transfer occurs, which means that more of the car's weight is supported by the front wheels. As the

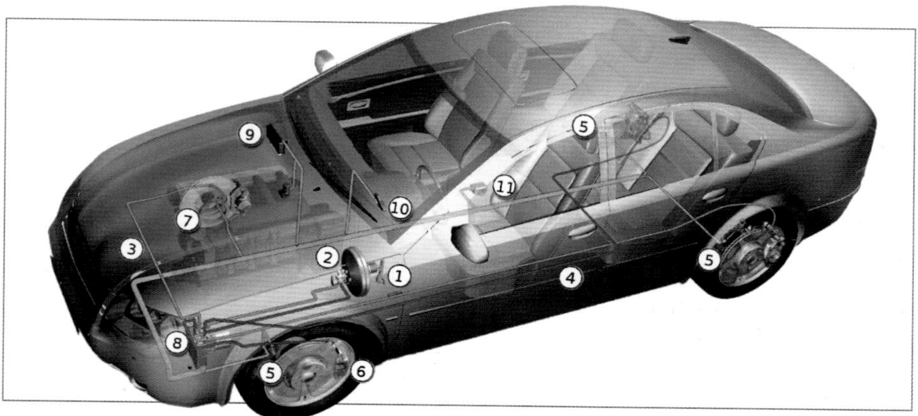

Fig 76: A modern braking system working in harmony with an electronic stability system to provide better car control and safety. 1 Brake pedal, 2 Brake booster (servo), 3&4 Brake lines, Wheel speed sensors, 6 Calliper, 7 Brake disc, 8 Electronic stability program's hydraulic unit with integrated electronic control unit, 9 Engine management unit, 10 Steering angle sensor, 11 Vertical axis angular velocity sensor. Blue and red lines are the dual braking hydraulic systems which each brake one front and one rear wheel. Yellow lines are wiring connections betwen various sensors and control units. (Courtesy Bosch)

front of the car gets heavier, the front brakes have more work to do.

Fig 76. A basic braking system consists of a brake pedal, parking brake system, hydraulic pressure cylinder (master cylinder), brake lines, and individual wheel brake assemblies (drums or discs). Nothing too sophisticated here, when the brake pedal is pushed, the movement is transferred to a piston in the master cylinder. This in turn pushes pressurised hydraulic fluid through pipes to smaller hydraulic cylinders at the wheels which either push friction shoes against the inside of the brake drum or push friction pads to clamp a brake disc.

The parking brake in most cases is completely mechanical. Through a series of cables and levers it directly locks the rear wheel brakes, or alternatively locks the transmission so that the wheels cannot turn.

The hydraulic pressure cylinder, also called the master cylinder, consists of a brake fluid reservoir and a cylinder with a piston inside. The piston is driven mechanically by the brake pedal. A dual master cylinder is a step up from the basic brake system. It has a secondary brake fluid reservoir with another piston, so that if the primary piston fails (mechanical problem or a brake fluid leak), the car can still be stopped.

Modern cars also have a brake booster (brake servo unit). A device that amplifies the hydraulic pressure you create with your foot. It looks like a drum and is mounted between the brake pedal mechanism and the master cylinder. Inside the drum there is a diaphragm with a vacuum control valve in the centre. When you push the brake pedal, the control valve closes and the diaphragm is pressed towards the master cylinder's piston, assisting its movement. The booster is powered by vacuum generated by the engine or a supplementary pump.

The master cylinder piston evenly

Fig 77: Typical wheel hub with disc and calliper. (Courtesy Chevrolet)

distributes hydraulic pressure through brake lines (narrow pipes) to disc brake callipers or drum brake wheel cylinders (slave cylinders).

Both disc brake pads and drum brake shoes have a friction lining. The lining is softer than the disc (or the drum), so friction wears this away rather than the disc or drum. When it is worn to a certain level, you can change the shoes or pads without doing any other repair work to the brakes.

Disc brake

Fig 77. A disc brake consists of a large metal disc and a stationary calliper with two opposing pads. When the brake pedal is depressed and pressure in the system increases, brake fluid fills the calliper's cylinders and pushes the pistons with the pads towards the disc. The disc – which is mounted on the wheel hub – is squeezed between the pads, and the resulting friction slows the car. When the brake pedal is released, slight eccentricity in the brake disc pushes away the friction pads.

In extreme cases, for really fast cars, there can be four pistons per calliper, allowing for pads with a much larger surface area.

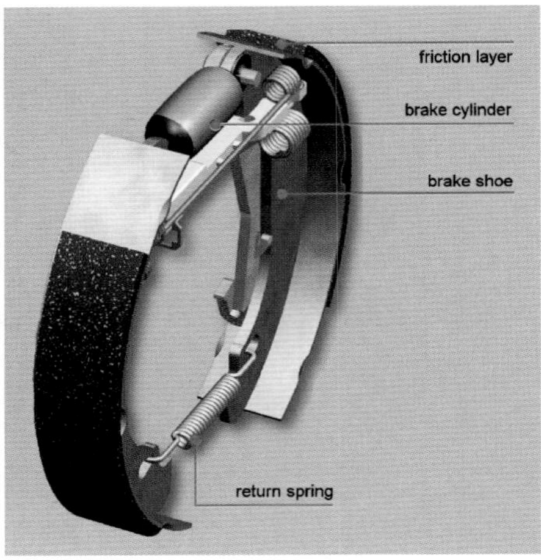

Fig 78. A simplified schematic of the internal components of a drum brake. These components would be mounted on a fixed backplate. The hollow brake drum fits over the components, so that the brake shoes can push against the drum's inner wall to create friction. (Courtesy Delphi)

Drum brake

Fig 78. A drum brake consists of a steel drum mounted on the wheel hub, and a brake shoe assembly mounted on a backplate fixed to the axle housing or the suspension upright. The brake line powers two small hydraulic cylinders (slave cylinders), attached to the brake backplate, and to the two shoes via piston arms. There are also systems employing a double cylinder (two pistons with two arms each powering a shoe), but these are not as efficient. When you depress the brake pedal, the shoes are pressed against the inner wall of the drum, and the wheel slows as a result of the friction created. When the brake pedal is released, springs pull the shoes back to their resting positions.

four

Electronics and safety

Car electronics

Today some cars can have up to 110 metres/ 120 yards of wiring inside – approximately the length of a football pitch. To help you make at least some sense of this sophisticated mesh of wire, they are all colour coded. For example, the wires powering headlights are likely to be white and blue.

The 'heart' of the car's electronic system is the battery. Although there are more modern and efficient options available, the lead-acid battery is here to stay for some time. It is very simple, cheap, and provides sufficient power our needs.

Electricity is distributed to the various systems through fuse boxes, the main one of which is usually located in the engine compartment or in the boot (trunk), with an additional one under the dashboard (but they can be almost anywhere). The main function of fuses is to safeguard the electronics and prevent fire. Fuses and coloured wiring also make it much easier to detect electronic faults, narrow them down to a particular circuit, and repair them quicker.

Onboard computer and entertainment system

The onboard computer or electronic control unit (ECU) is the brain of any modern car. As you may remember from chapter two, there are a huge number of sensors gathering information about engine temperature, exhaust gas content, etc. A car can be compared to a human, your fingers being sensors, and your nervous system the ECU. When you touch a hot surface with your finger, a signal is sent to your brain saying 'ouch!' This triggers a response from the actuators (muscles) and the finger is lifted back to safety. As the car has got no muscles, the role of the actuators is played by small electric motors, and electronic or hydraulic switches.

Fig 79: An older generation electronic control unit. (Courtesy Delphi and Ford)

With the advance of computer systems, the car computer – or 'carputer,' as it is amusingly called – has gone down in size, but has added so much brain power that it can now run various onboard systems and even communicate with the outside world. For example, some of the modern electric cars have a bluetooth or 3G mobile link that can send messages to your mobile phone with information about the battery level, or bring up data about the closest available charging points.

The carputer also governs the car's entertainment system, which today is much more than the archaic car radio. It is unbelievable what different and various devices a modern car entertainment system can contain. The CD player and CD changer are more or less obvious, but there can also be LCD TVs and DVD players for the rear seat passengers. MP3 players and gaming consoles? No problem!

However, the carputer also powers devices that are related to safety – parking sensors that beep when you roll too close to something, outboard video cameras that can replace the rear-view mirrors, and sometimes a global positioning system device, or GPS.
A large amount of GPS devices sold are aftermarket; you just stick them on the dashboard or windshield, and they don't actually interact with your car's ECU. Newer cars, however, come with an optional built-in GPS receiver to aid navigation.

Fig 80: A modern passenger wants to be entertained, even when travelling by car. (Courtesy Volvo)

How does a GPS work?

Fig 81. The abbreviation GPS refers to the system that makes the receivers work; the gadget that helps you find your way is called a GPS receiver, but it is often shortened to just GPS.

GPS is based on a network of 27 satellites orbiting the Earth about 12,000 miles from the surface. Each satellite makes two full journeys around the planet every day, receiving and transmitting radio signals. They are powered by large solar panels.

The system works on the principle of trilateration. Your GPS receiver needs to be in contact with at least three satellites to determine your current position. Each satellite knows its own co-ordinates (latitude and longitude), and your receiver knows how far it is from each satellite by measuring the speed at which the transmitted radio wave returns from it.

Trilateration works by eliminating all the possible places where you could be. If satellite A is 50 miles from your car,

Fig 81: A built-in, pop-up satellite navigation system. (Courtesy TomTom and Renault)

it doesn't help a lot. A huge number of places are 50 miles away from satellite A. If you draw a dot on paper, which will represent the satellite's location, and then draw a circle with a 50 mile radius, you can be anywhere on that circle.

But then the satellite B comes in play. Let's assume you're 40 miles from satellite B. Draw another circle that intersects your circle in two points. It means that your car is on one of those points. But which one? Here's where we need the help of satellite C – by getting the distance from a third satellite, we reduce all the possible coordinates to just one. The GPS receiver contains a database of streets and places that are linked to latitude and longitude. By getting your current coordinates and comparing them with its street database, the gadget tells you where you are and how to get where you want to go, turn by turn.

Onboard diagnostics and dashboard gauges

It is very important to monitor the dashboard and watch out for warning lights. Almost every car, even the basic ones, will have some sort of self-diagnosis system that can warn the driver of a possible fault. Red lights are warnings, yellow lights are cautions, green or blue lights shows that a certain unit is working.

On the very latest cars many of the

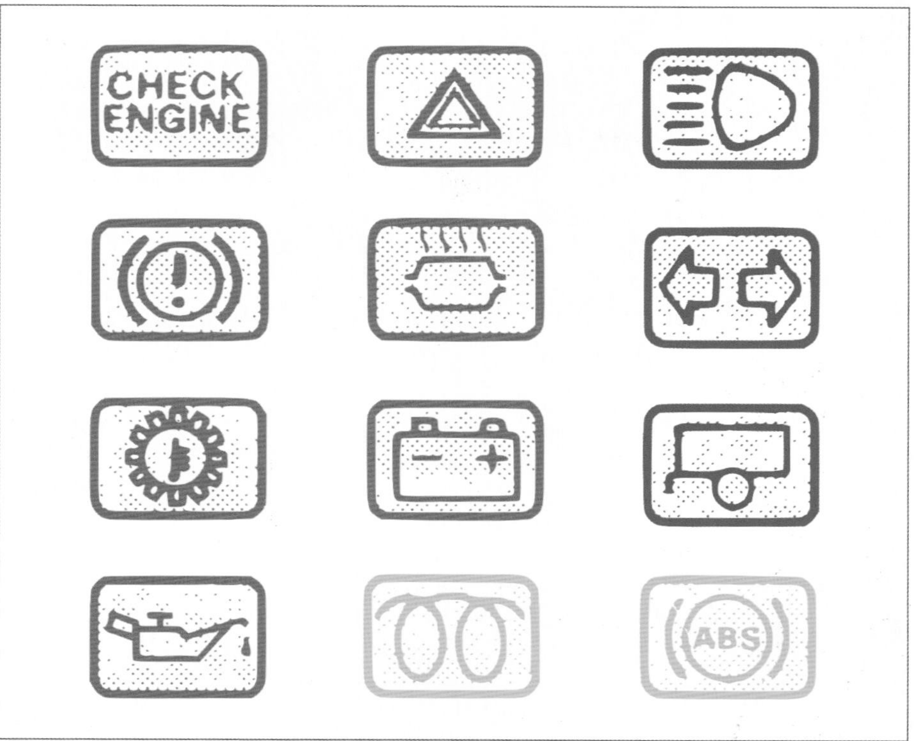

Fig 82: Dashboard information symbols.

dashboard lights have been replaced by a central LCD info screen, on which warning messages appear.

Red lights

- Check engine – if this comes on, you still have a chance to limp slowly to the service station. Ignoring this light is not really an option.
- Handbrake – this light should go out when you release the handbrake. If it comes on during driving and you're sure that you're not driving with the handbrake on, it may indicate that there's a fault in the braking system.
- Transmission oil temperature – this light can come on when you're towing a heavy trailer or demanding too much of your transmission. If it happens, just stop where it is safe and wait for it to cool down. If the light comes on regularly, suspect a fault.
- Low oil pressure – this light normally comes on when you turn on the ignition. However, when the engine is running, it should quickly switch off. If it doesn't, check the engine oil level. If it is filled to the correct mark, something is wrong with the lubrication system.
- Hazard warning light – flashes on and off when you turn on the hazard signal.
- Catalyst – comes on if the catalyst overheats. Catalysts don't normally do that, so it is definitely a fault.
- Battery low – this light usually comes on as a bulb check when you turn the

ignition on. When the engine is started, it should go out. If it stays on and you're confident that the battery is alright, it may indicate that something is wrong with the alternator.

• Some cars also warn about blocked filters, low fuel level, and faults in other systems.

Yellow lights

• ABS – the light goes off when you reach around 5mph. If it stays on, or if it comes on during normal driving, a fault is possible.

• Glow plug (diesels only) – this indicates that the engine is cool and the glow plugs need to be heated. The usual procedure is to wait for the light to go out before starting the engine; however, consult the car manufacturer's handbook for specific instructions.

Green or blue lights

• Headlights, direction indicators and trailer direction indicators only indicate that the respective light is on.

Air-conditioning and heating

Getting the temperature right inside the car is quite tricky.

Every car will at least have a heater, and the main part of such a heating system is the heater core – a small radiator tucked underneath the dashboard. Engine coolant is pumped through the heater core as it leaves the engine and makes its way to the main radiator at the front of the car. The heater core is enclosed in a plastic casing with several outputs. Large tubes connect the outputs to various areas in the car interior.

Air is forced through the tubes by a small electric fan. When the engine gets really hot, the air produced by the heater core gets hot as well – even too hot. It is therefore possible to feed cooler, outside air into the heater tubes, where it can be mixed with the hot air according to the adjustments that you've made to the heater controls on the dashboard. When you turn the heater control into the blue section, the heater core is covered and only outside air is fed into the car.

During the summer when using the fan to blow outside air into the car, the incoming air feels cooler than the actual outside temperature. This is because it is fed under low pressure (the fan builds up pressure in the tubes), and once the air escapes through the vent nozzles, it expands, causing it to cool. However, such a cooling method is very archaic and inefficient, which is why many cars come with an air-conditioner.

Fig 83. Air-conditioned cars still have the heater core and a system of tubes similar to the one described. However, the cool air won't be fed directly from the outside. Instead, it will go through the conditioner's system first. This can give you a breeze of really cool air in hot summer (and sometimes a sore throat and runny nose, too).

A basic air-conditioning system consists of a compressor, condenser radiator, receiver-drier, evaporator radiator, and an expansion valve. It works in a similar manner to a fridge or a dehumidifier. The compressor, which is driven by a belt from the engine's crankshaft, increases the pressure of the working coolant (Freon in most cases). As the pressure increases, so does the temperature, and Freon leaves the compressor as hot gas. Passing through the condenser radiator at the front of the vehicle, it is cooled by the oncoming air. The gas starts to condense and leaves the condenser as hot, high-pressure liquid.

The coolant is then passed through the receiver-drier, the main function of which is to take the moisture out of the

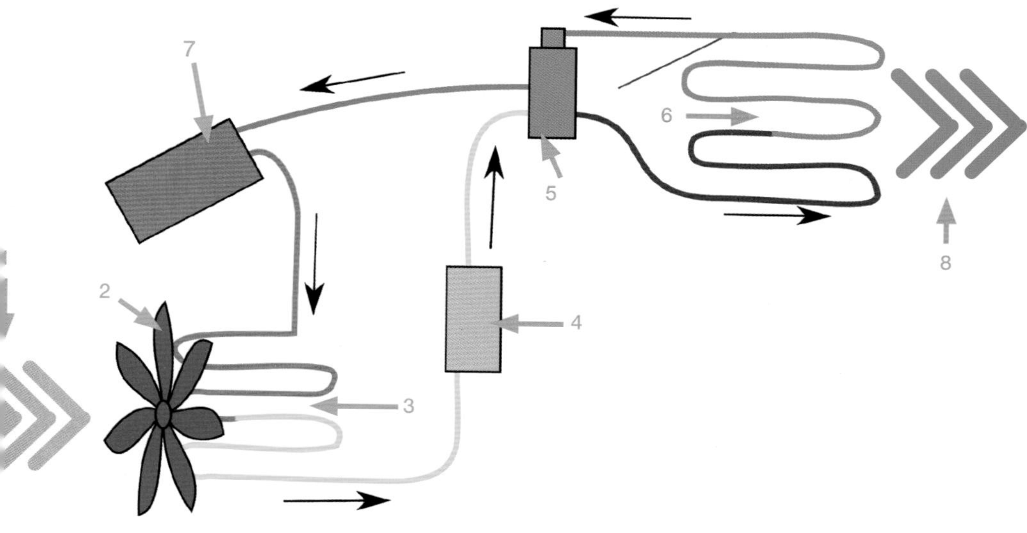

Fig 83: Simplified schematic of an air conditioning system.
1 Air at ambient temperature, 2 Fan, 3 Condenser, 4 Receiver/drier, 5 Expansion valve, 6 Evaporator, 7 Compressor, 8 Cooled air to passenger compartment. Black arrows show the circulation path of refrigerant and gases.

coolant and to ensure there's always plenty of coolant in the system. The receiver-drier contains a small canister of Freon, and tops up the coolant as necessary. The coolant passes through a special layer of desiccant (moisture absorbing granules) inside the receiver-drier that extracts moisture. This is important, otherwise the air conditioner tubes and radiators would suffer from corrosion. The desiccant should be replaced with fresh material at least once every two years.

The receiver-drier hasn't changed the condition of the coolant – it is still hot high-pressure liquid when it enters the low-pressure section of the expansion valve. The valve lets only a restricted amount of coolant through to the next level. Therefore, where the tube comes out of the valve a pressure drop is created, and the hot liquid begins turning back to gas.

As it enters the evaporator radiator, the pressure drops further and the Freon begins to boil. There's a peculiarity, though – it boils at -26ºC, and the radiator removes the heat from the air that is passing through it. So, as a result, no cold air is created in the conditioner – it simply takes the heat out of warm air. Now we simply have to deliver the cooled air into the interior of the car or mix it with the hot air from the heater core to create a suitable temperature.

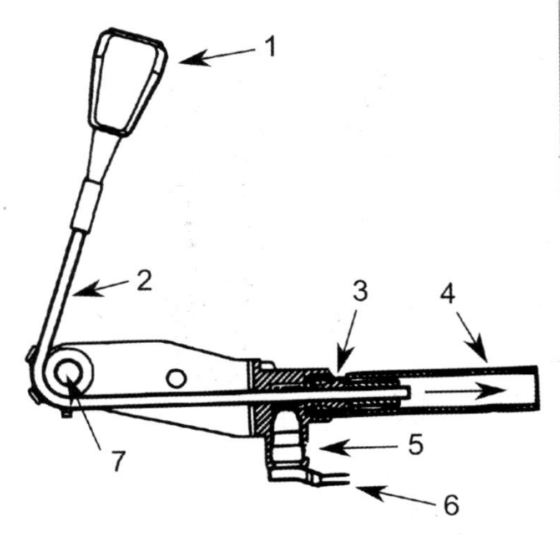

Fig 84: This safety belt tensioner is located at the fixed end of the seatbelt (1). When a sensor (6) detects an impact, an explosive charge (5) shoots the piston (3) backward in its housing (4), thus pulling the cable (2) around a wheel (7) to tension the belt, preventing the passenger from moving forward. (Courtesy Ford)

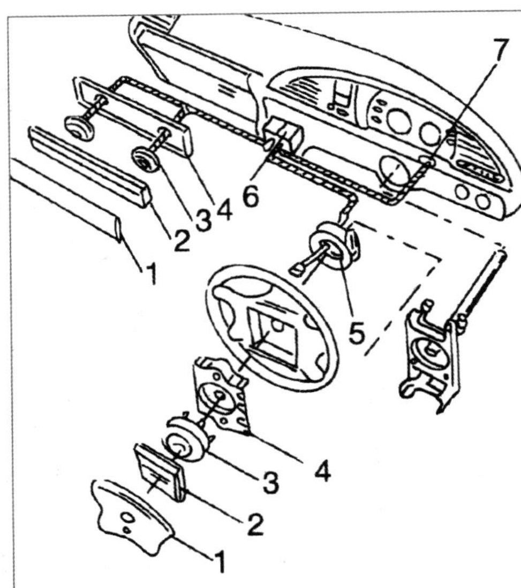

Fig 85: A simple schematic of an air bag system. 1 Steering wheel horn cover, 2 Tightly folded air bag, 3 Explosives container, 4 Housing, 5 Start spring, 6 Control unit, 7 Signal lamp. (Courtesy Ford)

Safety features

There's been a lot of effort and investment applied to making vehicles safer. Things that make the car relatively safe are divided into two large groups: passive safety features help passengers stay alive and well in an event of a crash; active safety features help drivers avoid accidents.

Passive safety

Safety belts

By far the simplest safety feature, and also the one that has saved the most lives. The safety belt prevents a person from crashing into the dashboard and flying through the windshield if the car hits an obstacle and comes to a sudden halt. It also restrains rear seat passengers. Remember that when a collision happens, your speed is the same as your car's – flying out of the car at 30mph is a terrifying prospect!

A seatbelt is wound onto a spool, and a spiral coil on the spool's body keeps the belt taut. When a sudden stop occurs, your body jerks the belt suddenly and triggers the stopping mechanism. The simplest of these is a pair of rollers that slip into a confined space, trapping the belt between them in the event of a strong jerking movement. The stopping mechanism can also be a ratchet with a loose sliding pin. When you move the belt slowly, it gives, but when the belt is jerked, the pin blocks the ratchet gear mounted on the spool.

Modern vehicles also use a pre-tensioner, usually located slightly below the belt spool. If a collision is

Fig 86: Air bags deployed in a left-hand drive Mercedes CLS. Although not shown, the headrail airbags on the passenger side would also be deployed. (Courtesy Mercedes)

sensed, a contained explosion pushes a rack upwards. The rack's gears engage with the spool's ratchet gear and turn the spool backwards, thus compensating for the distance that your body has already made from the moment of collision. An alternative form of pre-tensioning is shown in Fig 84.

Safety belts save tens of thousands of lives every year.

Airbags

The airbag system automatically inflates large nylon cushions, literally a split second after a collision occurs. Impact sensors are located at the front of the vehicle, and they react to a dramatic drop in speed or a direct impact. The sensors send a signal to the control unit, which deploys the airbags by causing a small explosion under the folded airbag and filling it with gas.

This all takes just 50 milliseconds (1/50th of a second), which is fast enough to cushion the car's occupants. The moment the head or body impacts the air bag, vent holes let the gas out progressively.

Figs 85 & 86. The front air bags are located in the steering wheel (under the centre cover) and near the glovebox. There may also be side-impact air bags that protect the heads and shoulders of driver and passengers during a side-on collision. Often there are frontal air bags for the rear passengers, incorporated into the backs of the front seats.

Fig 87: Crunch zones built into the car's body. These are designed to resist intrusions into the passenger compartment and to absorb energy. The corrugated members above the front wheel arches will collapse progressively (Courtesy Renault)

Crunch zones and body features

Fig 87. A very important passive safety feature is the way the car's body has been designed. Crunch zones are areas at the front and rear of the car, as well as in the doors, that will absorb the tremendous kinetic energy of a collision by changing shape or disintegrating.

Collapsable steering column

There are different types of collapsible steering columns, but the idea is more or less the same – to introduce a weakest link so that the steering column can collapse rather than being pushed into the car in a collision. A weakest link can be created near one of the universal joints, so that the joint breaks if necessary. A more unusual approach is to make one part of the column vulnerable by reducing the structural stiffness, e.g. it could be a section of latticed tube. It will still be able to turn the wheels, but when it comes under pressure it will disintegrate or collapse.

Active safety

ABS, or anti-lock braking system

• The purpose of ABS is to prevent wheels from skidding and to keep the wheels steerable, even on ice. If you brake with wheels that are about to lose their grip on the road surface, they will lock (stop revolving instantly), and you'll simply lose control and the car will go where it wants. The ABS system 'feels' when the wheels are about to start locking and prevents it by applying the brakes in short bursts. This braking is more efficient, and you can still steer the car.

Fig 76, chapter 3. ABS consists of speed sensors at each wheel, a pump, valves, and a control unit. The speed sensors send a signal to the control unit when the wheels stop spinning suddenly. When this happens, the control unit opens a valve located on the brake lines. The pressure is released and the brakes stop working. The pump then compensates the loss of pressure caused by the valve and the brakes are re-engaged. If the wheel continues to lock, the whole process is repeated until the car has safely stopped.

Good tyres

Although it sounds too simple to be true, tyres, when you get the right set, are the best active safety system available. Driving with a worn set or an inappropriate type of tyres is a surefire way to get into trouble. Drivers should follow car manufacturer's suggestions, and try to avoid cutting corners by saving money on tyres.

Hi-tech and futuristic safety systems

In the future, cars will become even safer. Many intricate safety systems have been invented, but they haven't yet found their way into mass production, mainly because it would be too expensive to implement them. However, sooner or later some of them will become basic equipment.

Parking sensors

Parking sensors are mounted at a car's extremities. They emit ultrasound, and measure the distance to the nearest obstacle by calculating the time it takes for the sound to reflect back from it. If it detects that another car or obstacle is too close, the parking sensor will beep loudly. This can be a very valuable guide, because many people struggle to 'feel' their car's dimensions.

Some high-end cars already come with parking sensors installed. The technology is neither overly expensive nor too sophisticated, and Do-it-yourselfers can buy a parking sensor kit for a modest price and install it on any car.

Collision avoidance

This idea is similar to that of parking sensors, but more complicated. The collision avoidance system uses a high-frequency radar to detect obstructions and objects in front of the car. The system can also have an additional sensor that will look out for red traffic lights and warn the driver. The majority of current collision avoidance systems use audible warning to get the driver's attention, but the latest generation systems have access to the vehicle controls, so if the driver fails to react to the signals, the system will actually hit the brakes or adjust steering automatically. Similar technology has been used on aircraft for decades, but it is only in the last couple of years that it has been applied to cars.

Only very few cars, including Mercedes, Volvo, Lexus and Infinity models, have such a system installed. Theoretically, it is possible to link a collision avoidance system with GPS, and create a car that drives on its own ...

Onboard drunk driving (DUI) test

Imagine a car that can tell if you've been drinking or not. Before starting the engine, the carputer will present a series of short DUI (driving under influence) tests where response reaction is measured. If the reaction is found to be too slow, the carputer switches off the main circuit and the car cannot be started. Many customer groups would find this device extremely insulting, and because it slows down the starting process, it is questionable whether the DUI tests will ever become mainstream, unless mandated.

Night vision

Fig 88. A night vision system incorporates an infrared camera at the front of the vehicle and a small LCD monitor on the dashboard. It would provide better visibility in fog and darkness by enabling the driver to see past the beam of the headlights. Again, not too expensive to implement, but car manufacturers are still trying to determine whether using night vision systems would actually reduce road risks.

Fig 88: Night vision system in operation. (Courtesy Bosch)

Pedestrian airbags

It is estimated that in one third of fatal human versus car collisions, the pedestrian dies of traumas caused by hitting the A-pillars (the pillars each side of the windscreen) and the windscreen. Therefore many companies have begun developing a pedestrian airbag system that will deploy external airbags on impact.

One of the most advanced systems has been invented at Cranfield University, England. The sensors are mounted at the front of the car, and when it is detected that the pedestrian has been hit, the bonnet (hood) will instantly pop up (to cushion the impact) and a U-shaped airbag will be inflated to cover the A-pillars and the bottom of the windshield. Low speed impact with the front of the car is not what causes fatalities (at worst it can result in a broken leg), so the airbags could make a lot of difference providing that the pedestrian falls off the bonnet the right way, onto the torso, not head first.

five

Help yourself

- A car is usually made to last a very long time. If maintained properly, it can easily survive for decades. There are habits that increase the life of your car significantly. Unfortunately, there are habits that do the very opposite. In fact, 'habit' is the keyword here. Form a set of good ones and you'll become a great motorist, and owning a car will become a pleasant experience.
- One of the most important habits to form is checking the warning lights before moving off. Not only will you spot possible faults before they get really bad, you'll also safeguard yourself from driving with an engaged parking brake.
- Make sure you are hundred per cent confident about which fuel should go in the car. If it's your own car, it's all pretty much self-explanatory ... one should hope, anyway. If it's a hire car or you've borrowed it, just ask. Thousands of motorists damage their cars every month just because they accidentally put the wrong fuel in. If you feed petrol (gasoline) to a diesel engine, it will strip all the lubricant and the engine will grind itself to death. Diesel fuel fed to a petrol engine will clog the fuel system and almost certainly put it out of action, along with the expensive catalytic converter. Although it may sound silly at first, it's a good idea to perform a reality check ritual before each fill-up. As you lift the nozzle, repeat to yourself the fuel type that is displayed on the nozzle. Then ask yourself what type of fuel required for this vehicle? This 'foolish' little method could save us an aggregate fortune every year.
- Keep and maintain a full service history of your car. Not only does this increase the resale value of your vehicle, it also gives you a complete picture of what's gone on, keeps maintenance under control and ensures longevity for your car.
- Keep a diary to remind yourself when it is necessary to change the engine oil, transmission oil, and other

fluids, or when the next service is due if you have it done for you. In fact, changing oils and filters is the one of the cheapest and simplest of maintenance procedures so many drivers do it themselves. Well oiled and maintained cars seldom require serious and expensive repair work – that's a fact.

• Make sure you change the filters and fluids at regular intervals. Filters are far cheaper than serious repairs.

By the way, changing filters and engine oil is not exactly what one would describe as rocket science. So, if you enjoy doing some DIY, see if you can carry out these simple jobs yourself. This could easily save you a considerable sum every year.

• Be gentle with the clutch. This will increase the working life of both the clutch and the transmission.

• Check the tyre pressures every week and keep them at the pressures recommended by the car manufacturer. Check that the tyres are not damaged at the same time.

• Check the coolant and washer bottle levels every week. A continual loss of coolant indicates a problem that needs to be investigated.

• Always pay attention to unusual noises and smells. The car is a big noisy thing, that's true, but you should never assume that a new noise appearing is just how things are.

• It is important to release the ignition key as soon as the engine starts. By turning the key you engage the electrical circuit, and the starter motor turns the flywheel. You should also take care not to accidentally turn the key into the starting position with a running engine. It will inevitably damage the starter's gear as it hits the spinning flywheel.

• Opening the hood/bonnet with the engine running is extremely dangerous. The rotating fan can cause severe injuries. If you have to open the hood with the engine still running, make sure you tuck your hair under a hat, and remove your tie or any other loose garment that could be trapped by the fan. Mind your fingers too.

six

Glossary of terms and units

Bhp

Brake horsepower is the power measure at the engine output, without considering the power loss inside the transmission and drive. Horsepower was introduced by James Watt to provide a reasonable comparison between a horse's power and a steam engine's power (in order to sell more engines to miners). Sir James determined that a horse can raise 330lb of coal out of a 100ft mine in one minute. It was rather inaccurate. However, horsepower stuck, and it is a term that we can all relate to and use to compare various engines. Although EU directives have banned the use of horsepower in an attempt to eradicate all imperial measurements, nobody really seems to care. For the record, one horsepower is 0.7457kW. You may have also seen sources listing 'brake horsepower' – this also refers to the power generated by the engine (as measured on a dynamometer). If the word 'brake' is omitted, we're probably talking about power to the wheels (power loss occurs in the transmission and drive). Incidentally, an adult male human can produce 1.5 to 2.5hp for a short period of time.

Coefficient of drag (Cd)

A figure that measures the air resistance created by a car's profile. The lower the figure, the better. A streamlined body has a lower air resistance – basically, this means less power is needed to displace air as the car travels through it.

Large, boxy cars have a Cd of 0.40 or more. An average sedan will be around 0.28. Reducing Cd by just a fraction (0.01) will give you an extra 0.2 miles per gallon. Probably the lowest ever Cd of a four-seater is 0.17, achieved by the Solectria Sunrise electric car in 1998.

Miles per gallon

A measure of how economical your

internal combustion engine-powered car is. According to today's standards 30mpg is pretty normal, but much depends on engine size, car weight and driving techniques.

Miles per kWh

A measure of how economical your electric car is. A modern electric car consumes around 0.25kWh of electricity per mile.

Power

The amount of work performed by your engine during a certain period of time.

Torque

A force that creates rotation. Torque is the moment of force (leverage at point where force is applied), relating to an object turning around its axis. It is measured in Newton-metres (Nm) or pound-feet (lb ft). 1lb ft is equal to 1.356Nm. It is especially important at low speeds. You get the most torque out of your engine when in first gear. For quick acceleration and successful off-roading, high torque is absolutely essential.

Also from Veloce –

ISBN: 978-1-845843-10-6 • Paperback • 21x14.8cm • £12.99* UK/$24.95* USA • 128 pages • 67 colour and b&w pictures

What if we all had to say goodbye to petrol cars tomorrow? Would you be ready? This book will help you find out. With a concise catalogue covering the best production models and the most promising prototypes, this book is the definitive guide to the future of motoring.

*prices subject to change, p&p extra.
For more details visit www.veloce.co.uk or email info@veloce.co.uk

Also from Veloce –

ISBN: 978-1-845843-51-9 • Paperback • 21x14.8cm • £9.99* UK/$19.95* USA • 96 pages • 32 colour pictures

This book describes in a clear, friendly manner everything today's driver needs to know about choosing and using a car in an economical and eco-efficient way. Includes helpful information on alternative fuels, hybrid powertrains, and much more.

*prices subject to change, p&p extra.
For more details visit www.veloce.co.uk or email info@veloce.co.uk

Also from Veloce –

ISBN: 978-1-845843-96-0 • Paperback • 21x14.8cm • £9.99* UK/$19.95* USA
• 96 pages • 120 pictures

Aimed at the driver who wants to do his or her own basic car maintenance and servicing without the need for in-depth mechanical knowledge, or a technical manual. A must-have for all drivers.

*prices subject to change, p&p extra.
For more details visit www.veloce.co.uk or email info@veloce.co.uk

Index